First World War
and Army of Occupation
War Diary
France, Belgium and Germany

15 DIVISION
Headquarters, Branches and Services
General Staff
21 September 1915 - 13 October 1915

WO95/1911/6

The Naval & Military Press Ltd
www.nmarchive.com
Published in association with The National Archives

Published by

The Naval & Military Press Ltd

Unit 10 Ridgewood Industrial Park,

Uckfield, East Sussex,

TN22 5QE England

Tel: +44 (0) 1825 749494

www.naval-military-press.com

www.nmarchive.com

This diary has been reprinted in facsimile from the original. Any imperfections are inevitably reproduced and the quality may fall short of modern type and cartographic standards.

© **Crown Copyright**
Images reproduced by permission of The National Archives, London, England, 2015.

Contents

Document type	Place/Title	Date From	Date To
Heading	WO95/1910-4a 15 Div HQ Gen Staff & Depts Sep 1915- Apps [21-30 Sep		
Heading	Reports on Operations. 21st-30th September, 1915. 15th Division And Units.		
Miscellaneous	1. General Staff.		
Miscellaneous	Report On The Operation From September 21st To September 30th, Inclusive.	05/10/1915	05/10/1915
Miscellaneous	Casualties Suffered By The 15th Division For The Period 25th, 26th, and 27th September.	25/09/1915	25/09/1915
Miscellaneous	2. Medical.		
Miscellaneous	Report Of Operations From 21st to 30th September. Medical Services 15th Division.		
Miscellaneous	Colonel G.F. Rawnsley, C.B., D.S.O., R.A.M.C. Casualties Sufferd by The 15th Division For The Period 25th, 26th, & 27th September.	25/09/1915	25/09/1915
Miscellaneous	3. R.E. & Signals.		
Miscellaneous	Report by C.R.E. 15th Division on Work performed by R.E. Units 21st to 30th September 1915	01/10/1915	01/10/1915
Miscellaneous	R.E. (2) 15th Division.	02/10/1915	02/10/1915
Miscellaneous	Squares	01/10/1915	01/10/1915
Diagram etc			
Diagram etc	Arrangements for Visual Communication		
Miscellaneous	4. 11th Motor Machine Gun Battery.		
Miscellaneous	Report from 11th Motor Machine Gun Battery-Operation September 21st to 30th, 1915	02/10/1915	02/10/1915
Diagram etc	Sketch-Not To Scale		
Miscellaneous	5. 15th Divisional Cyclist Company.		
Miscellaneous	15th Divisional Cyclist Coy Report On Action 25th 26th And 27th Sept.	01/10/1915	01/10/1915
Miscellaneous	6. 15th Divisional Mounted Troops.		
Miscellaneous	Report on Operation Feb 24-28. 15th Div Mounted Troops		
Miscellaneous	7. "F" Trench Mortar Battery.		
Miscellaneous	Report on Operation Sep 24-28 F. Trench March Battery		
Miscellaneous	8. 44th Infantry Brigade.		
Miscellaneous	Report on attack on 25th September 1915	02/10/1915	02/10/1915
Miscellaneous	Casualties 25th. 26th, 27th Sept 44th Infantry Brigade.		
Miscellaneous	9. 45th Infantry Brigade.		
Miscellaneous	45th Brigade-15th Division. Report on Operation from 21st September to the 30th September, both dates inclusive.	01/10/1915	01/10/1915
Miscellaneous	10. 46th Infantry Brigade & Units.		
Miscellaneous	Report of 46th Infantry Brigade on Operation between 21st and 30th September.	21/09/1915	21/09/1915
Miscellaneous	Operations 25/26th Reference Trench Map Sheet 36.c. N.W.		
Miscellaneous	A Attach On Hill 70. 25/9/15 Part 1.	25/09/1915	25/09/1915
Miscellaneous	Part 2.	25/09/1915	25/09/1915
Miscellaneous	Narrative	28/09/1915	28/09/1915

Miscellaneous	No 5 Column 12 H.L.I. Report on Operation of A. and B. Companies and M.G. Section 12th Bn High. L.i. during attack 25th and 26th September.		
Miscellaneous	Head Quarters A 6th Inf Bde.	13/10/1915	13/10/1915
Miscellaneous	Report of the O.C. No. 5 Column 25th And 26th September 1915	07/10/1915	07/10/1915
Miscellaneous	12th. H.L.I. Short Narrative of events 25th/26th Sept. 1915.	29/09/1915	29/09/1915
Miscellaneous	85 K O S A	28/09/1915	28/09/1915
Miscellaneous	Report by Major H. Pollard-Lowsley C.I.E., R.E. on the Operation of the 24th to 27th inst.	29/09/1915	29/09/1915
Miscellaneous	Report by Captain A.P. Sayer R.E. 91st Field Company R.E. on Operation from 24.9.15 to 27.9.15	28/09/1915	28/09/1915
Miscellaneous	A Form Messages And Signals.		
Miscellaneous	91st Field Coy RE.	29/09/1915	29/09/1915
Miscellaneous			
Miscellaneous	11. 9/Gordon Highlanders (Pioneers).		
Miscellaneous	9th Gordons Commanding 9th Gordon Highlanders, (Pioneers).	01/10/1915	01/10/1915

WO95/1910-4a

15 Div HQ Gen Staff et Depts

Sep 1915 — Apps [21-30 Sep]

R E P O R T S   O N   O P E R A T I O N S.

21st - 30th September, 1915.

15th DIVISION AND UNITS.

1. GENERAL STAFF.
2. MEDICAL.
3. R.E. & SIGNALS.
4. 11th MOTOR MACHINE GUN BATTERY.
5. 15th DIVISIONAL CYCLIST COMPANY.
6. 15th DIVISIONAL MOUNTED TROOPS.
7. "F" TRENCH MORTAR BATTERY.
8. 44th INFANTRY BRIGADE.
9. 45th INFANTRY BRIGADE.
10. 46th INFANTRY BRIGADE & UNITS.

       (A)   10/Scottish Rifles.
       (B)   7/K.O.S.B.
       (C)   12/H.L.I.
       (D)   12/H.L.I.
       (E)   8/K.O.S.B.
       (F)   91/Field Co. & "H" Co. 9/Gordons.
       (G)   91/Field Co.
       (K)   91/Field Co.

11. 9/GORDON HIGHLANDERS (Pioneers).

1. GENERAL STAFF.

REPORT ON THE OPERATIONS FROM SEPTEMBER 21st
TO SEPTEMBER 30th, INCLUSIVE.

1.   Copies of Operation Orders (the last of which were issued on September 21st) were sent to the Fourth Corps at the time of issue.   None of these are therefore attached to this report.

2.   Preparations for the attack were completed by the night of September 20th;   these included:-

(a)   The digging of about 8 miles of new communicating and reserve trenches, the latter provided at intervals with splinter-proof cover.

(b)   The construction of deep dug-outs for Advanced Divisional, Divisional Artillery, three Brigades and Divisional R.E. Head-quarters.

(c)   The provision and stocking of 7 grenade stores, 4 S.A.A. Stores and 2 R.E. Stores in the forward trenches, and of a central R.E. Stores and S.A.A. Depot in QUALITY STREET.

(d)   The placing of 10 water tanks and a large number of barrels and petrol tins in the support trenches, and the improvisation of a large regular water supply at FOSSE 7.

(e)   Construction of 28 bridges for the passage of guns and transport through the system of trenches.

(f)   The multiplication and safe laying of telephone wires and the provision of visual signal stations.

(g)   The construction of Advanced and Divisional dressing and collecting stations at FOSSE 7, QUALITY STREET, LE PHILOSOPHE and MAZINGARBE;   and of regimental aid posts and a central evacuation trench.

(h)   The laying of a tramway from MAZINGARBE to LE PHILOSOPHE, FOSSE 7 and QUALITY STREET for the conveyance of stores

and

and the evacuation of wounded; and the construction of trucks.

(i) The construction of recesses in the front parapet for the gas cylinders, and the conveyance of 996 cylinders into the trenches.

(j) The laying out of a special Divisional road from VAUDRICOURT to MAZINGARBE for passage of troops.

(k) The exact mapping and labelling of all trenches in the area.

(l) The construction of three Russian saps towards the enemy's front line.

(m) The placing of one day's iron ration for the Division in the CORONS DE FOSSE 7.

The above work, together with other minor preparations, was carried out with unremitting energy by the Divisional R.E. working with the 9th Gordon Highlanders (pioneers). The labour demanded from the infantry was great, and was cheerfully and effectively given.

5. The bombardment commenced on September 21st and continued up to the hour of assault on September 25th; during this period the front trenches were lightly held.

The enemy's reply was weak, increasing slightly on the third and fourth days.

The wire on the enemy's front and support trenches was difficult to observe, but was examined nightly by patrols and proved to be well cut. A demonstration by the Divisional Artillery at 4 p.m. on September 23rd drew weak hostile rifle and machine-gun fire.

Our own wire on the front of our assault was cut in diagonal strips on the night of September 23rd/24th.

The

3.

The preliminary moves of the Division were completed by the evening of September 23rd; and at 4 p.m. on the 24th Advanced Divisional Head-quarters moved to MAZINGARBE (next door to Divisional Artillery Head-quarters), the 2nd echelon moving to NOEUX-LES-MINES.

At 8.5 p.m. on the 24th the message to "carry on" was received from Advanced IVth Corps, and brigades began moving into their forming-up places.

At 11 p.m. information was received that IVth Corps Operation Order No. 35 for the attack held good.

4. The troops of the Division were in their forming-up places by 2 a.m. on the 25th. The whole of the infantry and R.E. of the Division were thus formed up underground on a front of 2,000 yards and a depth of 3,000 yards.

At 3.35 a.m. instructions were received that the hour of zero = 5.50 a.m., and all concerned were informed.

5. At 5.50 a.m. the discharge of gas and smoke commenced; the morning was dull, with slight rain; the wind light and varying from S.S.W. to W. The weather conditions were thus not very favourable for an attack by gas.

At 6.30 a.m. precisely the assault was launched.

6. The casualties from shrapnel and machine-gun fire were heavy on leaving our front trenches, but the assault was not checked. The effect of the gas on the enemy's front line was disappointing; the smoke candles provided an effective curtain for covering the assault.

At 6.50 a.m. our infantry were reported to be through the enemy's support trench; and ten minutes later the third lines of the assaulting columns were reported as crossing the German front trench. The reserve (45th) Bde. had begun to move

forward

forward without difficulty. The smoke was still very thick, making observation difficult.

By 7.40 a.m. the whole of the assaulting columns of both leading brigades had left our trenches, and the brigade reserves were in our front line preparing to follow. The leading troops of the 44th Brigade had reported at 7.5 a.m. that they were approaching LOOS.

The 180th (Tunnelling) Co. R.E., less two sections already forward, was now ordered up to LE SAULCHOY FME from VERQUIN.

At 9 a.m. the probability of our left being attacted against PUITS 14 Bis owing to the delay of the 1st Division became apparent; a message was therefore sent to Advanced IVth Corps suggesting that the H.A.R. should bombard the strong points in H.25 and H.31 previously indicated to them. This was done.

At 9.25 am. a report was received from 73rd Brigade R.F.A. that they had seen our infantry advancing through G.36.b and G.30.d at 9.10 a.m.

8. At 9.30 a.m. orders were issued through the C.R.E. to prepare crossing places for the cavalry and artillery over our own and the German front line trenches. This task was allotted to the 74th Field Co. assisted by the 180th Co. A portion of the latter company had already been placed at the disposal of the Divisional bombing officer for the transport of grenades to the assaulting brigades.

At the same time the C.R.A. was instructed to move up two batteries to positions of readiness at FOSSE 7.

Our infantry were now reported to be in PUITS 14 Bis and advancing up Hill 70.

9. At

5.

9.   At 9.50 a.m. the greater part of the leading brigades were through or past LOOS; and the 45th (reserve) Brigade was in our front line trenches, less one battalion which had moved on in support of the 44th Brigade.

As the advance had gone so fast, the C.R.A. was now instructed to arrange to group the 70th Bde. R.F.A. with the 44th Infantry Brigade and the 71st Bde. R.F.A. with the 46th Infantry Brigade, and brigades were so informed.

This grouping was cancelled again in the evening.

10.   At 10.20 a.m. the 1st Division reported that their 2nd Brigade was hung up in front of the German front trench by the wire, and asked that a battalion from the 45th Bde. be detached to work northwards to assist. The great extent of ground now covered by our own troops did not admit of the detachment of a battalion for this purpose. The grenadiers of the 6th Camerons were, however, ordered to bomb northwards and rendered great assistance in relieving the situation.

The 46th Infantry Brigade reported Hill 70 taken at 10.10 a.m. and estimated the casualties of the brigade at 10 per cent.

11.   The 45th Infantry Brigade were now ordered to push forward their leading battalions on the right and left into the German front line trenches, but no further.

As a matter of fact the right battalion had already gone forward unknown to the Brigadier.

At the same time the 11th M.M.G. Battery was ordered to QUALITY STREET to come under the G.O.C. 44th Infantry Bde. and to be pushed forward to LOOS at his discretion.

Later on orders were sent for this battery to report to 46th Infantry Brigade. The Battery Commander was unable to

do

6.

do this, but went right forward on his own initiative, and rendered valuable service in assisting to hold the line on Hill 70.

12. At 11 a.m. the G.O.C. 46th Infantry Brigade reported his left in PUITS 14 Bis and his right pushing on to CITÉ ST. AUGUSTE; he reported his left quite exposed and his No. 5 column (half battalion 12th H.L.I., which connected with the 2nd Bde.) checked in the German front trenches and suffering heavily.

A battalion of the 45th Infantry Brigade (6th Camerons) were immediately ordered forward to his support, directed with their right on PUITS 14 Bis.

At 11.15 a.m. the C.R.A. was instructed to arrange with the H.A.R. to lift their barrages previously arranged to N.1.d, N.2.c, N.2.d, and 1000 yards E. of the German trenches on the west of ST. AUGUSTE, and H.26.d.3.6 to north and east.

General McCracken explained the situation by telephone to the Corps Commander, and earnestly pressed for the forward movement of the Army reserves.

At 11.30 a.m. the Divisional Squadron was moved up to join the cyclist company at MAZINGARBE, and the IVth Corps were informed that only two battalions now remained in hand as Divisional Reserve.

13. At noon there were no signs of the approach of other troops to reinforce the Division. The 44th and 46th Infantry Brigades were reported to be holding Hill 70, but unable to progress against CITÉ ST. AUGUSTE; The losses amongst the troops who had pushed on over the Hill were heavy; and the left flank was exposed owing to the failure of the 1st Division to advance. The 45th Infantry Brigade (less the battalions already detached) was therefore ordered to push on to LOOS and hold it, and release the troops of the 44th and 46th

Infantry

Infantry Brigades to go forward. The H.A.R. were requested to bombard for a complete period of half an hour the trenches and CITÉ of ST. AUGUSTE; and at 12.40 p.m. the two companies 9th Gordons (pioneers) in reserve were ordered up to LOOS to put it in a state of defence.

14. At 1.40 p.m. the G.O.C. 21st Division and G.O.C. 62nd Brigade arrived at Divisional Head-quarters. The former did not remain to discuss the situation but wrote some message and immediately left again. At 2 p.m. a message was received from Advanced IVth Corps ordering 21st Division to Advance on LOOS via FOSSE 7 and to place the leading brigade at the disposal of 15th Division.

Soon after 2 p.m. the G.O.C. 62nd Brigade returned and the situation was explained to him by General McCracken. Verbal orders were given him to move his brigade by QUALITY STREET to LOOS; to get into touch with the G.Os.C. 44th and 45th Infantry Brigades; if Hill 70 was lost to retake it; if held, to relieve our troops on it; if situation favoured a further advance on CITÉ ST. AUGUSTE, to act accordingly in co-operation with 44th and 45th Infantry Brigades. He then left. These orders were then confirmed in writing, and sent after him. He was also provided with some trench maps, which he did not appear to possess. He said nothing about the state of his brigade.

The subsequent movements of this brigade are difficult to follow. The leading battalion was reported as reaching QUALITY STREET at 3.30 p.m., but it seems probably that at least one other battalion went more to the south and arrived at LOOS Cemetery. The Brigadier on his return on the 27th reported that he never got touch with his battalions, though

he

8.

he himself met the G.Os.C. 44th, 45th, and 46th Infantry Bdes. Traces of the doings of his battalions are recorded in the reports of the Brigadiers of this Division, which are attached.

Bde.-Maj. 62nd Bde. appeared at Divisional Head-quarters at about 7.30 p.m., received an account of the situation as far as it was known, and the orders given below in para. 16, was provided with maps, and went off again to find his Brigadier.

15. At 2.30 p.m. 44th Inf. Bdes reported mixed bodies of our troops entrenching on the reverse slope of Hill 70 from H.31.b.6.6 to H.31.a.7.2, and at 3.15 p.m. 44th Inf. Bde. H.Q. moved forward to LOOS.

At 4 p.m. 1st Division reported the capture of the Germans who were holding up the 2nd Brigade; at 4.40 p.m. the 2nd Brigade was reported moving forward, and the anxiety as to our left flank was lessened.

16. At 6 p.m. orders were issued to brigades to consolidate their positions from Hill 70 to PUITS 14 Bis connecting up with 47th Division on the right and 2nd Brigade on the left; 45th Infantry Brigade to relieve 44th Infantry Brigade on slopes of Hill 70, the latter to withdraw behind LOOS into Divisional Reserve; 62nd Brigade to place one battalion at disposal of 46th Infantry Brigade and to hold remainder in support of 45th and 46th Infantry Brigades about PUITS 15. These orders were duly acknowledged by all brigades, but apparently the 62nd Brigade were unable to comply.

17. The situation at the close of the 25th was as follows:- The Crest of Hill 70 and the work on top of it were in German hands. A mixture of the troops of the 44th, 45th and 46th Infantry Brigades were digging themselves in below the crest;

the

9.

the line extended to PUITS 14 Bis, which was still held by us. Major Wace, G.S., went down to LOOS in the afternoon and there met all brigadiers in the course of the evening. He was able to explain the situation and materially assist them. During the night the 44th Infantry Brigade was withdrawn to our own trenches.

The general tendency of the advance had been to the south-east towards the CITÉ ST. LAURENT, rather than due E. This can only be accounted for by the attraction of the natural features, and by the heavy fire which came from the neighbourhood of the DYNAMITIERE. In many of the reports sent in the CITÉ ST. AUGUSTE was mentioned in mistake for the CITÉ ST. LAURENT. This tendency to drift south-east was very marked all through the operations.

18. At 9.7 p.m. orders were received from Advanced IVth Corps that the division was to be prepared to resume the offensive on the 26th and the 2nd Brigade was placed under our orders. This latter provision was revoked two hours later, and the 2nd Brigade ordered to rejoin its own Division west of BOIS CARRÉE.

General McCracken explained to the Corps Commander on the telephone the state of the division and his doubts as to its fitness to resume the offensive.

19. At 11.30 p.m. a telephone message was received from Advanced IVth Corps that the division assisted by the 62nd Brigade would attack Hill 70 at 9 a.m. on the 26th after one hour's intense bombardment.

At 1.45 a.m. on the 26th an order was received confirming this message, and orders were issued for the attack to be carried out by the 45th and 62nd Brigades.

20. At

10.

20. At 12.30 p.m. the enemy delivered a counter-attack on the right battalion of the 45th Infantry Brigade which was repulsed by machine-gun fire.

At about 5.30 a.m. the enemy delivered another and heavier counter-attack from the south-east which was repulsed.

At 8 a.m. the bombardment of Hill 70 commenced and was very accurate. At 9 a.m. the assault was delivered and came under heavy machine-gun fire from the S.E. corner of the DOUBLE CRASSIER, and under the fire of our own artillery.

The assault failed; was renewed, and failed again. The 62nd Brigade in support, it is stated, did not come on. Had they done so, the G.O.C. 45th Infantry Brigade considers that the attack would have succeeded, as the enemy were reported to be evacuating the Redoubt.

A request was sent at 8.35 a.m. to 47th Division to be ready to assist with one battalion. A battalion was told off by the 47th Division for this purpose, but the 141st Brigade failing to get into touch with the 45th Infantry Brigade, this assistance was not forthcoming.

21. At about 10 a.m. the situation began to be critical. The retirement of other troops affected the men of the Division, who, being mostly without officers, began to retire. The G.O.C. 46th Infantry Brigade, some of whose men were on the hill, greatly distinguished himself by rallying men and taking them back, and in this work he was ably assisted by Capt. Sayer, R.E. and other officers. The men of the 15th Division responded at once, and the original line was retained; the men of the 62nd Brigade could not be rallied.

22. The situation remained much the same till noon, when an attack delivered by another brigade on our left (presumably of

21st

21st Division) against the CITÉ ST. AUGUSTE broke in disorder under shell fire and retired from the field. This increased the difficulty of holding the line on Hill 70, which began to break; and apparently it was about this time that PUITS 14 Bis was lost. The men, however, responded to every effort to reform them, and, with the assistance of some 100 volunteers of his own and the 45th Brigade sent forward by G.O.C. 46th Infantry Brigade, the line was reinforced about 5 p.m. and maintained.

23. At 2.35 p.m. the 6th Cavalry Brigade (less one regt.) was placed at the disposal of the Division and pushed forward into LOOS to hold it at all costs with the remaining troops of the Division still there. The remainder of the 46th and 44th Infantry Brigades with the Divisional Squadron and a platoon of cyclists were ordered to hold the old line of German front trenches between the LENS ROAD REDOUBT and the LOOS ROAD REDOUBT, both inclusive.

At 3.30 p.m. the G.O.C. 6th Cavalry Brigade arrived in LOOS and was placed in command of the troops there. The wireless set and pigeons were handed over to him, and 45th Inf. Bde. H.Q. withdrew to QUALITY STREET. All available officers were sent to LE PHILOSOPHE to collect stragglers, and take them forward to our old front trenches. Several hundreds of men of the 21st Division were collected in this way.

At 6.30 p.m. owing to reports received chiefly from the 46th Infantry Brigade that our troops were still holding on to the line on Hill 70, orders were sent to G.O.C. 6th Cavalry Brigade to get into touch with them and reinforce them. Arrangements were made at the same time for the establishment of a barrage of artillery fire to cover them. This barrage was very effective.

24. At

24. At 10.30 p.m. orders were received from Advanced IVth Corps for the 62nd Brigade to rejoin its Division. The remnants of it were therefore collected and sent away.

At 12.25 am. on the 27th orders were issued, in accordance with instructions from Advanced IVth Corps, for the withdrawal of the Division (less artillery) to MAZINGARBE. This was carried out without incident.

At 3.45 p.m. orders were issued for the move of the Division on the 28th to DROUVIN - HOUCHIN - HAILLICOURT.

At 11.30 p.m. the mounted troops were warned to be ready to move at an hour's notice - apparently forward - Nothing happened and the order was subsequently cancelled.

On the 28th the Division moved to the area allotted - one-third of the infantry bivouacked in the open - Headqrs. moved to DROUVIN.

On the 29th Headqrs. moved to LABUISSIERE.

On the 30th one brigade at HAILLICOURT was ordered to move out to make room for the French; it marched to LABUISSIERE and BRUAY.

25. Reports of my Infantry Brigadiers, C.R.E., O.C. Signal Co., O.C. 9th Gordons (pioneers), Divisional Squadron, Cyclist Co., M.M.G. Battery Commanders, and A.D.M.S. are attached. I consider these reports too valuable to be omitted and they are too detailed for inclusion in my own report.

The Divisional Artillery worked throughout under the orders of the IVth Corps, and will doubtless render their report direct. Brig.-Gen. Alexander worked in the closest co-operation with me throughout the operations and rendered valuable service.

The

13.

The work done by the artillery in cutting the wire during the preliminary bombardment, in supporting the attacks, and in placing barrages of fire where required was conspicuously good. The First Group H.A.R. also rendered prompt and effective assistance whenever called upon.

26. I consider that none of my elaborate preliminary preparations were wasted. The division was launched to the attack under the most favourable conditions, the casualties up to the time of the actual assault were negligible, the supply of grenades, ammunition and tools was well maintained, and the large numbers of wounded were attended to and evacuated with despatch.

27. Communications throughout were very good. Except for very short intervals, communication between Division and Brigade Headquarters was maintained by telegraph and telephone during the whole period under report. The wireless and pigeon service proved very valuable in keeping up communication with LOOS. The work of the Divisional Signal Co. was excellent; it was owing to their efforts, and to the frequent reports sent in by artillery observers, and by the officers actually engaged, that I was kept in close and constant touch with the situation.

28. Between 14,000 and 15,000 grenades were taken into action on the men. These proved very useful and materially assisted the advance. The grenadiers of all battalions showed conspicuous courage and resource.

29. The Lewis machine-gun proved a serviceable weapon. The machine-gun detachments greatly distinguished themselves

and

14.

and their losses were heavy. The 11th M.M.G. Battery also rendered most valuable service.

30. I am of opinion that the arrangements for discharging the gas require more organization and study. A number of cylinders remained undischarged, and a good deal of gas found its way into our own trenches.

I suggest that the cylinders should be connected up in batteries, and manipulated from well under cover; also the discharge pipes should be buried in the parapet to prevent their being blown back into the trench by shells.

The smoke candles were very effective. But a holder on a long stick is required for them, so that the candlemen can keep well under cover.

The discharge of gas drew a heavy artillery fire on our front trenches.

31. I have no hesitation in saying that had fresh troops of good quality been held in readiness to follow closely on the heels of my Division, the German line would have been pierced. My Division carried out its orders to the letter, at great speed, and exhausted itself in the effort. The Division sent to support me came too late, and was not in a condition fit to enter such a fight. Its Commander and Staff appeared quite unfamiliar with the ground or the situation and made no effort to get into close touch with me or my Staff. No member of the Staff of the Guards Division or of the XIth Corps came near my Headquarters, though the G.O.C. 3rd Cavalry Division kept in constant touch with me.

It is beyond my province to suggest that the task allotted to the Divisions or Corps destined to support my attack required as careful preparation and previous study

as

15.

as did the task of my Division.   But I must beg permission to point out that these precautions were apparently lacking, and to deplore the result.

My orders to push on to the full extent of the power of the Division were clear and definite and were carried out to the full in the confident assurance that the promised flow of reinforcements behind me would be maintained.   In the event, I consider that nothing but the high soldierly qualities displayed by officers and men of my Division averted a disastrous retreat from the positions won.

32.   I cannot close this report without paying a tribute to the discipline, bravery and resource shown by all ranks under my command.

The spirit of officers and men remains high in spite of the heavy losses sustained, and the fighting value of the division will be completely restored as soon as reinforcements of personnel and material are received.

The following appendices are attached:-

App. 1.	Total Casualties.	
,, 2.	Report - G.O.C.	44th Bde.
,, 3.	,, ,,	45th Bde.
,, 4.	,, ,,	46th Bde.
,, 5.	,, of C.R.E.	
,, 6.	,, of O.C. 9th Gordons.	
,, 7.	,, O.C. Divl. Squadron.	
,, 8.	,, of O.C. Cyclist Co.	
,, 9.	,, of M.M.G. Battery.	
,, 10.	,, of O.C. Signal Co.	
,, 11.	,, of A.D.M.S.	

5th Oct. 1915.

(Sd) F.W.N. McCracken, Maj.Gen.,
Comdg. 15th (Scottish) Division.

CASUALTIES SUFFERED BY THE 15th DIVISION FOR THE PERIOD 25th, 26th, and 27th SEPTEMBER.

Units.	OFFICERS.					OTHER RANKS.				
	Killed.	Wounded.	Missing.	Gassed.	Total	Killed.	Wounded.	Missing.	Gassed.	Total
H.Q. 44th Bde.	-	-	1	-	1	-	-	-	-	-
9th Black Watch.	8	11	1	-	20	68	314	292	5	679
8th Seaforth Hrs.	5	10	4	-	19	44	362	294	-	700
10th Gordon Hrs.	-	5	2	-	7	23	221	130	-	374
7th Cameron Hrs.	4	6	4	-	14	64	255	215	-	534
13th Royal Scots.	6	9	1	-	16	37	224	105	4	370
7th R.S. Fus.	6	11	1	-	18	63	240	83	-	386
11th A & S Hrs.	7	4	1	-	12	36	214	64	-	314
6th Cameron Hrs.	8	8	-	1	17	30	270	70	-	370
7th K.O.S.Bs.	9	7	3	-	19	12	221	404	-	648
8th K.O.S.Bs.	3	7	4	-	14	23	124	228	4	379
10th Sco. Rifles.	12	5	4	-	21	68	318	239	-	625
12th H.L.I.	7	11	-	-	18	59	184	315	-	558
9th Gordon Hrs. (Pioneers).	5	4	-	-	9	21	179	64	4	268
70th Bde.R.F.A.	-	2	-	-	2	1	12	-	-	13
71st ,, ,,	-	-	-	-	-	1	14	2	2	19
72nd ,, ,,	-	1	-	-	1	-	1	-	-	1
73rd ,, ,,	-	-	-	-	-	2	8	-	-	10
11th M.G.Batt.	-	2	-	-	2	-	3	-	-	3
15th Divl.Cyclists.	-	-	-	-	-	1	6	-	-	7
73rd Fd.Co.R.E.	2	2	1	-	5	10	14	29	-	53
74th ,, ,,	-	-	-	-	-	3	3	1	10	17
91st ,, ,,	-	-	1	-	1	9	32	11	-	52
45th Fd.Amb.RAMC.	-	-	-	-	-	-	4	-	-	4
46th ,, ,,	-	1	-	-	1	-	1	-	4	5
47th ,, ,,	-	-	-	-	-	-	3	-	-	3
Totals.	82	106	28	1	217	575	3227	2546	41	6389
Attached Units.										
180 Co. R.E.	-	-	-	-	-	1	22	2	-	25
187 ,, ,,	-	-	-	-	-	-	1	-	4	5

2. MEDICAL.

REPORT OF OPERATIONS FROM 21st to 30th SEPTEMBER.
MEDICAL SERVICES 15th DIVISION.

Reference:- MAP BETHUNE COMBINED SHEET 1:40,000.

REGIMENTAL AID POSTS.

These were situated in the trenches as follows:-

44th INFANTRY BRIGADE.
1. Near Quality Keep South in communication with Communication Trench No.2, which will be kept open for conveyance of wounded only. (Medical Officers 10th Gordons and 7th Camerons).
2. In the new Communication Trench No.36. This Communication Trench will be for wounded only. The Dressing Station is on the S. side of this trench a few yards W. of trench "21". (Medical Officers 9th Black Watch and 8th Seaforths).

46th INFANTRY BRIGADE.
1. Just E. of the junction of "21" and new Communication Trench.
   (Medical Officer 10th Scottish Rifles).
2. Close to I.
   (Medical Officer 7th K.O.S.B.)
3. In "14A" just W. of junction with "26".
   (Medical Officer 12th H.L.I.).

2.

46th INFANTRY BRIGADE (continued).

4. (a) In "15" just W. of junction with "Northern Up".
   (b) In "14" just W. of junction with "15".
   ((a) and (b) are alternative positions.)
   (Medical Officer 8th K.O.S.B.).

UNITS R.A.M.C.

The R.A.M.C. units employed were the 45th, 46th and 47th Field Ambulances, and the 32nd Sanitary Section R.A.M.C. Territorial Force.

DISPOSITION.

The above units were located as follows :-
45th FIELD AMBULANCE.

1. ADVANCED DRESSING STATION.

THE ABATTOIR, MAZINGARBE.

At the Abattoir 4 capacious dugouts were prepared each capable of sheltering 12 lying down cases. Access to 2 of these was by a doorway and steps leading from the interior of the building. These 2 dugouts were connected to 2 others by means of a trench 6 feet broad and about 50 yards long. This was provided with seats on one side for a portion of the way capable of affording accommodation for about 50 sitting cases. A fifth dugout across the road afforded shelter for 12 lying cases.

The Abattoir itself had lying accomodation for 200 cases.

3.

2. REST POST, MAZINGARBE.

At the Brewery MAZINGARBE and the CHATEAU next to it.

The above buildings gave housing for 200 lying down and about 300 sitting cases.

3. MAIN DRESSING STATION was located in the following buildings NOEUX-LES-MINES.

(a) Divisional Bath House.
(b) A school house containing 4 large rooms.
(c) A barn with 2 large divisions.
(d) The Mairie buildings.

The above buildings were able to house 400 lying down cases.

The total accommodation thus provided was therefore

	lying	sitting
1. At ADVANCED DRESSING STATION.	260	50
2. At REST POST	200	300
3. At MAIN DRESSING STATION.	400	200
Total	860	550

46th FIELD AMBULANCE.

1. ADVANCED DRESSING STATION.

48 Houses and Cellars at QUALITY STREET.

	lying	sitting.
Accomodation.	350	150

2. REST POST & DIVISIONAL COLLECTING STATION. located at BREWERY, PHILOSOPHE.

Capacious cellars were protected from shell fire by sand bags above the roof, and propped up inside with beams to bear the extra weight thus superimposed. Electric light was laid on.

4.

Accomodation here provided was for

	lying	sitting
	200	100

3. MAIN DRESSING STATION.

In converted barns and tents at VAUDRICOURT.

	lying	sitting
Accomodation	300	400

Total accomodation provided thus was :-

	lying	sitting
1. ADVANCED DRESSING STATION.	350	150
2. REST POST & DIVISIONAL COLLECTING STATION.	200	100
3. MAIN DRESSING STATION.	300	400
Total.	850	650

47th FIELD AMBULANCE.

1. ADVANCED DRESSING STATION.

FOSSE NO.7

Shelters were provided against the fosse and protected from shell splinters and shrapnel fire.

	lying	sitting
Accomodation.	120	120.

2. MAIN DRESSING STATION.

Located in 2 Schools at NOEUX-LES-MINES.

	lying	sitting.
Accomodation.	400	300

5.

	lying	sitting
Total accomodation was		
1. ADVANCED DRESSING STATION.	120	120
2. MAIN DRESSING STATION.	400	300
Total.	520	420

The 32nd SANITARY SECTION.

The Officer Commanding and 9 N.C.Os. and men did duty with 47th Field Ambulance and 1 Serjeant and 10 men with 46th Field Ambulance, at the Divisional Collecting Station. All ranks volunteered for this duty which was quite distinct from the service they enlisted for.

MAINTENANCE.

All posts were well lighted and equipped with Medical and Surgical material and food, kitchen and water.

METHOD OF EVACUATION.

Special communication trenches were told off for carriage of wounded only from Regimental Aid Posts to the Advanced Dressing Stations at FOSSE 7 and QUALITY STREET as follows :-

1. New Communication Trench No. 36
2. Communication Trench No. 2, and
3. Communication Trench No. 6 was also available

A tramway line was constructed running from QUALITY STREET and FOSSE 7 to the breweries at PHILOSOPHE and MAZINGARBE. It was for this reason that REST POSTS had to be provided at the termini at these places. The small trucks used at the Colliery were refitted with wooden

The Main Dressing Stations of the 47th Field Ambulance at NOEUX-LES-MINES and the 46th Field Ambulance at VAUDRICOURT were open also on the evening of 20th September. The 45th Field Ambulance opened its Main Dressing Station at NOEUX-LES-MINES on 24th September.

Up to the morning of September 25th. the daily casualty list of wounded was as follows :-

21st September	1
22nd September	9
23rd September	11
24th September	19
25th September to 6 a.m.	26
Total.	66

On the evening of September 24th the strength of the Advanced Dressing Stations was increased as follows :-

FOSSE 7 by 2 bearer subdivisions of 47th Field Ambulance.

QUALITY STREET by 2 bearer subdivisions of 46th Field Ambulance.

DIVISIONAL COLLECTING STATION by 1 N.C.O. and 10 men of the 32nd Sanitary Section R.A.M.C. Territorial Force.

On the morning of 25th September the Infantry assault was preceded at 5.50 a.m. by a gas and smoke attack; at 6.30 a.m. the infantry stormed the enemy's trenches with the bayonet and Casualties very shortly began to arrive at the Advanced Dressing Stations. The process of clearing the field worked well; as the troops advanced the Regimental Medical Establishments followed up forming new aid posts in more advanced positions, contact was well maintained between these Regimental Stretcher Bearers and those of the bearer divisions of the 46th. and 47th Field Ambulances; the wounded unable to walk were conveyed by stretcher carriage to the Advanced Dressing Stations at FOSSE 7 and QUALITY STREET. The Tramway from the Advanced Dressing Stations worked to the Divisional Collecting Station at PHILOSOPHE and by this means the wounded were rapidly evacuated, those able to walk followed in most cases the branch of the tramway to MAZINGARBE and were admitted to the REST POST and Advanced Dressing Station of the 45th Field Ambulance at this place.

From PHILOSCPHE Brewery evacuation was by the 21 Motor Ambulance Vehicles of the Divisional Field Ambulances, and the Sanitary Section Motor Lorry, to the Main Dressing Stations of the 45th and 47th Field Ambulances at NOEUX-LES-MINES and of the 46th Field Ambulance at VAUDRICOURT. The Motor Ambulance Vehicles also cleared on Saturday QUALITY STREET and FOSSE 7 by day, but on Sunday owing to heavy shell fire they were driven back and were unable to clear from there until the evening.

The horse ambulance wagons and general service wagons cleared from the Divisional Collecting Station and Stations at MAZINGARBE to all the Main Dressing Stations.

On Saturday afternoon 25th September I sent on, a bearer subdivision of the 46th Field Ambulance under Lieutenant J.R. Turner R.A.M.C. to LOOS to endeavour to bring in wounded from there. He went forward collecting them, but his party was subjected to shell fire and was also gassed by asphyxiating shells. This Officer was subsequently wounded and admitted to a field ambulance.

On Sunday 26th September I ordered C Section 45th Field Ambulance to proceed to LOOS and there open a Dressing Station. The section opened one in a house at G.34.d.6.9. on the LOOS Road and collected wounded until Monday at noon 27th September when they were shelled out of it. The Officer in charge, Captain H.R. Friedlander, R.A.M.C., was badly gassed but had all his wounded removed by stretcher carriage to QUALITY STREET. He remained behind and endeavoured under heavy shell fire to put his horses in the vehicles and bring them away. Several horses were killed and others stampeded, and the equipment was left. He showed very great gallantry on this occasion.

The casualties in the division during the course of the operations were enormous. I think I am correct in saying that they exceeded those on any previous occasion during the war. The figures speak for themselves. The admissions were as follows :-

21/9/15 to 6 a.m. 25/9/15.	66
6 a.m. to noon 25/9/15.	153
Noon 25/9/15 to noon 26/9/15.	2434
" 26/9/15 " " 27/9/15.	1662
" 27/9/15 " " 28/9/15	448
Total	4763

Some of the above casualties were amongst men of other divisions but none the less the work entailed by the Field Ambulances was the same; the number of these was 889.

The total of casualties of the 15th Division reported as admitted into other divisional Field Ambulances was 423.

The total of the 15th Divisional Casualties accounted for, was thus the large number of 4297 of all ranks.

With the exception of about 100 cases all the casualties admitted to our Field Ambulances, which meant 4600 cases, had been collected, their wounds dressed, and all ranks fed and housed by Sunday 26th September at midnight. It was obviously impossible to accommodate such large numbers in the Field Ambulances, so the difficulty was overcome by billetting the lighter cases, which entailed much extra work for the Medical Establishments.

Owing to the blocking of the roads by troops the
Motor Ambulances Convoy was unable to clear
sufficiently to do very much to ease the pressure
on the Field Ambulances until the evening of the
27th September. The task therefore of
maintaining and redressing the wounded had thus
to be continued until Monday 27th September.
The work of clearing the battlefield of wounded
had been done so rapidly and well that on the
morning of the 27th I was able to place at the
disposal of the Director of Medical Services
1st. Army, 14 Motor Ambulances to assist the
Motor Ambulance Convoys on the line of
communication in evacuating wounded.
Evacuation by No.8 Motor Ambulance Convoy from
the 27th September was rapid and by the 29th
all cases had been sent to Casualty Clearing
Stations except 48 mild gas cases which remained
in the 46th Field Ambulance on 30th September.
The scheme for removing the wounded worked
admirably and it is entirely due to the zeal and
devotion to duty of all ranks both of the
Regimental Medical and Field Ambulance
establishments that such splendid results were
obtained, and the battlefield was cleared of
4600 casualties by Sunday night.
I cannot praise their services too highly; all
ranks worked night and day for three days.
In conculsion I should like to place on record
the heroism displayed by the wounded which
lightened the task of those who had to minister

to them. No murmur or groan was heard amongst
this vast assembly of stricken heroes, many
with grievous wounds, joking and making light
of them, and cheering up their wounded comrades.
It was an honour appreciated by all ranks
of the Medical Service to serve such men.
In closing this report I wish to place on record
the courageous and devoted services rendered to
the British Army by Mdlle. Emilienne Moreau,
the particulars of which were furnished me by
Captain F.A. Bearn R.A.M.C., Officer in Medical
charge 9th Black Watch. This girl, who is only
17½ years old, was living with another woman in
a shop at LOOS in the Church Square. These
premises were taken as a Regimental Aid Post by
Captain Bearn and these two women spent the
whole day and night (25th - 26th September)
in helping to carry in the wounded and carry
out the dead, also in preparing food and coffee
for all, refusing payment. This work was done
continuously for 24 hours.

When the British Troops were making ineffective
efforts to dislodge 2 German Snipers from the
next house, who were firing on the stretcher
bearers, this young girl seized a revolver from
and officer and went into the back of the house
and fired two shots at the Snipers. She came
back saying "C'est fini" and handed the revolver
back to the officer. It is uncertain if the
two shots actually killed the men but the

13.

diversion in the rear enabled our men to effect an entrance in front.

Captain Bearn states - "I saw many examples of cool courage that day but none that excelled hers".

(Sgd). G.T.RAWNSLAY (?)

Colonel,
A.D.M.S 15th Division.

COLONEL G. F. RAWNSLEY, C.B., D.S.O., R.A.M.C.

CASUALTIES SUFFERED BY THE 15th DIVISION FOR THE PERIOD

25th, 26th, & 27th, SEPTEMBER.
1915.

UNITS	OFFICERS					OTHER RANKS				
	Killed	Wounded.	Missing.	Gassed.	Total	Killed	Wounded	Missing	Gassed	Total
Hd.Qrs.44th Bde.	-	-	1	-	1	-	-	-	-	-
9th Black Watch	8	11	1	-	20	68	314	292	5	679
8th Seaforth Hrs.	5	10	4	-	19	44	362	294	-	700
10th Gordon Hrs.	-	5	2	-	7	23	221	130	-	374
7th Cameron Hrs.	4	6	4	-	14	64	255	215	-	534
13th Royal Scots.	6	9	1	-	16	37	224	105	4	370
7th R.S.Fusrs.	6	11	1	-	18	63	240	83	-	386
11th A.& S. Hrs.	7	4	1	-	12	36	214	64	-	314
6th Cameron Hrs.	8	8	-	1	17	30	270	70	-	370
7th K.O.S.Bs.	9	7	3	-	19	12	221	404	-	645
8th K.O.S.Bs.	3	7	4	-	14	23	124	228	4	379
10th Sco. Rifles.	12	5	4	-	21	68	318	239	-	625
12th H.L.I.	7	11	-	-	18	59	184	315	-	558
9th Gordon Hrs. (Pioneers).	5	4	-	-	9	21	179	64	4	268
70th Bde. R.F.A.	-	2	-	-	2	1	12	-	-	13
71st Bde. R.F.A.	-	-	-	-	-	1	14	2	2	19
72nd Bde. R.F.A.	-	1	-	-	1	-	1	-	-	1
73rd Bde. R.F.A.	-	-	-	-	-	2	8	-	-	10
11th M.M.G. Batty.	-	2	-	-	2	-	3	-	-	3
15th Divl. Cyclists.	-	-	-	-	-	1	6	-	-	7
73rd Fld.Coy. R.E.	2	2	1	-	5	10	14	29	-	53
74th Fld.Coy. R.E.	-	-	-	-	-	3	3	1	10	17
91st Fld.Coy. R.E.	-	-	1	-	1	9	32	11	-	52
45th Fld.Ambl.R.A.M.C.	-	-	-	-	-	-	4	-	-	4
46th Fld.Ambl.R.A.M.C.	-	1	-	-	1	-	1	-	4	5
47th Fld.Ambl.R.A.M.C	-	-	-	-	-	-	3	-	-	3
	82	106	28	1	217	575	3227	2546	41	6389

UNITS	OFFICERS					OTHER RANKS				
	killed	Wounded	Missing.	Gassed.	Total.	Killed	Wounded	Gassed	Missing	Total
ATTACHED UNITS										
180 Coy. R.E.	-	-	-	-	-	1	22	-	2	25
187 Coy. R.E.	-	-	-	-	-	-	1	4	-	5

These are Hd. Qrs. figures and not the A.D.M.S.

3.   R.E. & SIGNALS.

Report by C.R.E. 15th Division on Work performed by
R.E. Units 21st to 30th September 1915.

Preparatory Work.

1. All the important work in the preparation of our trenches to enable an assault to be delivered from them had been completed before the 21st September, and the special stores collected and prepared by the R.E. for the Infantry Brigades had been issued.

21st to 23rd September.

2. The 73rd and 91st Coys R.E. were employed under the 44th and 46th Inf.Bdes respectively in adding finishing touches to trenches and providing additional splinter proof protection in the forming up trenches.

Advanced dressing stations and first aid posts were completed by these units during this period.

The 74th Coy was concentrated at NOEUX LES MINES and employed on the completion of road diversions and the provision of extra water supplies for R.A. horses in their advanced positions.

24th Sept.

3. During the evening of this day the 74th Coy moved to LE SAULCHOY FARM, MAZINGARBE with one section at the advanced R.E. Store at QUALITY STREET.

The 73rd and 91st Coys moved up to their forming up places preparatory to assault under Brigade orders.

The 180th (Tunnelling) Coy (less one section) came under the orders of the C.R.E. and were located :- H.Q. and one section at LE SAULCHOY FARM, MAZINGARBE, remainder with mechanical and horse transport at L.14.a.9.8 in readiness to move up at short notice when required.

The C.R.E. moved his H.Q. to LE SAULCHOY FARM.

25th Sept.

4.
(a) The 73rd and 91st Coys took part in the assault under Brigade orders.

Half of each company accompanied the assaulting columns of their respective Brigades (one section to each column) the other half of each company moved with the Brigade supports. Parties from each company were detailed to lay

out /

-2-

out and superintend the digging of communication trenches from our front line to the German front line trenches.

(b) The two leading sections of the 73rd company reached the ridge of HILL 70 with the leading infantry, both the officers and a large proportion of other ranks had become casualties before reaching LOOS. These two sections remained on the crest of HILL 70 until driven back to a line below the crest where they assisted the infantry to entrench. They were withdrawn about 10 p.m. by order of the G.O.C. 44th Infantry Brigade, but a part of No.2 Section remained behind all night and helped to hold the line.

(c) The remaining half company remained behind the Brigade supports until these advanced. While waiting some trenches over the LENS road were bridged, and while employed on this work one officer and ten men were killed and wounded. This half company followed the 10th Gordons to LOOS and proceeded to HILL 70, the crest of which was reached about 9.30 a.m. Finding some infantry in the Keep hard pressed they advanced to it and endeavoured to hold it. All were driven out and retiring behind the crest line began to dig in.

(d) A party of ten R.E. only under Capt Cardew, again advanced and managed to enter the keep but were driven out. They then assisted the infantry to entrench on the slopes of HILL 70 until withdrawn during the night. About 10 men remained all night assisting to hold the line.

(e) Of the leading sections of the 91st Company one (No.3) lost its officer at the commencement of the assault. After assisting infantry to turn the German support trench they proceeded to HILL 70. A barn at G.36.b.8.7 was placed in a state of defence. This section was subsequently combined with No.4, the other leading section which had advanced too far to the left towards that portion of the German trenches which was still held by them. This section suffered heavy losses, and, being unable to advance was ordered to withdraw.

They /

-3-

They were extricated by their officer who displayed the greatest gallantry in rescuing all his wounded under very heavy fire.

(f) The remainder of the Company did good work in the neighbourhood of HILL 70 and PUITS 14 Bis, assisting infantry to entrench, fortifying some houses and localities and preparing machine gun emplacements. They also assisted to hold the line on HILL 70.

(g) About 9.30 a.m. the 74th Company sent forward to prepare three artillery routes over the German trenches into LOOS and subsequently to near G.30.a. and c.

The routes prepared were :-

    (i) BETHUNE-LENS Road.

    (ii) VERMELLES-LOOS Road.

    (iii) A track in prolongation of a line of bridges previously prepared over our own trenches between (i) and (ii).

(h) The 180th Company were ordered to assist the 74th Coy in the above work. A portion of this company was placed at the disposal of the Divisional Bombing Officer and was employed in the transport of bombs to the assaulting Bdes.

(i) At 5 p.m. information was received that our Infantry were entrenching on HILL 70, and five pontoon wagons loaded with picks, shovels, sandbags, wire, etc were sent to LOOS and placed at disposal of 45th Infantry Brigade.

26th Sept. 5.
(a) The 73rd Company which had lost all its officers except the Commanding Officer, was ordered back to MAZINGARBE by the G.O.C. 44th Infantry Brigade. Having been reorganised into two sections it rejoined the 44th Infantry Brigade at QUALITY STREET early in the afternoon. This Company, although very exhausted, worked on improving the LENS Road from midnight 26th/27th until the work was completed about 4 a.m. on the 27th.

(b) Two sections of the 91st Company were ordered back to

MAZINGARBE /

HAZEBROUCK during the afternoon to rest, but an order being received for every available man to be sent up to the German front trenches they were ordered up again after a very short rest and assisted in collecting numerous stragglers and getting them into the trenches. The remaining portion of the company remained in the neighbourhood of Hill 70 and LOOS during the day, assisting the infantry by every possible means, by holding portions of the firing line, improving trenches, collecting and reforming stragglers, and in certain cases were instrumental in checking the retirement of infantry and saved a complete withdrawal from Hill 70.

(c) All available men of 74th and 180th Companies were employed until about 11 a.m. on improving the LENS Road which was in a very bad condition owing to having been much cut up by shell fire and by trenches dug across it, its condition being rendered worse by the heavy rain which had recently fallen.

(d) At 10.40 a.m. orders were sent to 74th Company to concentrate all these parties near our old front line trenches, to be prepared to block the communication trenches which connected our lines with the German lines and to prepare and restore and improve our wire. All these parties subsequently assisted to prepare the German front and support trenches for defence under the orders of G.O.C. 46th I.B.

(e) The detached section of the 180th Company R.E. rejoined during the afternoon and was also employed on this work. All remaining tools in HAZEBROUCK were sent forward for the use of the troops and stragglers collected in these trenches.

(f) During the night the C.R.E. proceeded to LOOS to

/inspect

inspect the road, and at midnight the 74th and 73rd Companies, although all very exhausted, were ordered out to do further work on the road which was made passable for motor ambulances by about 4 a.m. on the 27th.

27th September. 6. The Infantry Brigades having been withdrawn the three Field Companies concentrated at LE SAULCHOY Fm, MAZINGARBE. The 180th Company were ordered back into billets at VERQUIN and came under orders of the 4th Corps.

28th September. 7. All units withdrew from MAZINGARBE.

8. During the whole period from 21st September, four men of the 74th Company were employed on water supply duties in Fosse 7 until relieved on the evening of the 28th.

9. The total losses reported during the period under report were:-

  73rd Fd. Coy.   5 Officers.   50 Other Ranks.
  74th Fd. Coy.   14 Other Ranks.
  91st Fd. Coy.   1 Officers   51 Other Ranks.
  180th (T) Coy.   17 Other Ranks.

The Field Companies went into action with six officers and about 140 other ranks each.

10. Special cases of gallantry and good work are being brought to notice in a separate report. All reports received from independent sources testify to the extremely high standard of discipline, bravery, coolness and resource displayed by all ranks.

                (sd) G.S.CARTWRIGHT.

                    Lt.Col.R.E.,

1/10/15.   C.R.E., 15th Division.

R.E.(2).

15th Division.

In forwarding the attached A.F. W.3121 in connection with the recent operations, I wish to bring to notice the good work carried out by R.E. Companies in the 15th Division, viz:- 73rd, 74th and 91st Field Companies, also the 180th Company, which was attached to the Division before and during this period.

Preparatory Work. In the preparation of the trenches prior to the assault, the following works were carried out by and under the supervision of the R.E. companies and 9th Gordon Hdrs. aided by large infantry working parties:-

Communications.-

Communication trenches - Northern Up, Southern Up - extension of 12 - 12.A, 22, 23, 29, 31, 32, 16.a., extension of 6, 9.X., and 8.d.

Reserve Trenches.-

Trenches 20 and 21 with a certain number of bays provided with splinter proof covers.

No.24 Reserve Trench.

All trenches were labelled and boards with numbers provided at all junctions, etc., an evacuation trench for the wounded was dug during the 3 last days before the bombardment.

83 recesses were constructed in the parapet of the front trench for gas cylinders.

3 Russian Saps were run out to assist in connecting up the German trenches with our own system after the assault, these had just before the bombardment been carried about 40x to 60x out.

Advanced report centres for 2 Divisional and 3 Brigade Headquarters were provided with bomb-proof shelters.

/A

A trench tramway was laid to assist in the transport of stores from MAZINGARBE to QUALITY STREET.

3 Advanced Dressing Stations were installed at Fosse 7, BREWERY PHILOSOPHE. and ABATTOIR, MAZINGARBE.

Some 26 bridges were built over trenches to allow of transport proceeding along the road and Artillery crossing the trenches.

A number of regimental first aid posts were made in the trenches - off the evacuation trench and near the junction of main communications.

Store depots were also formed in the trenches and in QUALITY STREET and trestle wagons were held in readiness to push forward wire, sandbags, tools, etc., should the opportunity arise.

The reserve store was formed in MAZINGARBE.

Water Supply.

This presented many difficulties but owing to the ingenuity of 2/Lt. Evans and the hard work and perseverance of some 8 or 9 men of the 74th Company, R.E., a pump driven by a petrol engine was made up out of assorted machinery taken out of various places. This pumped about 2,000 gallons per hour out of a well 100 feet deep in Fosse 7. Storage in the trenches was provided by placing 10 galvanised tanks in the reserve trenches and also about 300 petrol tins.

The dressing stations were also provided for in the same manner.

During Operations.
In the attack on 25/9/15, the 73rd Field Coy with "G" Coy, 9th Gordon Highlanders (Pioneers) was with the 44th Brigade, the 74th Company, R.E., 2 Companies (E and F) 9th Gordon Highlanders (Pioneers) and 180th (Tunnelling) Coy, R.E.

/in

in Divisional Reserve and the 91st Field Coy R.E. with "H" Company 9th Gordons with the 46th Brigade.

All ranks displayed great gallantry in carrying out their duties and although they seem to a large extent to have joined in the fighting, yet whenever required they carried out such R.E. works that were called for such as the supervision of the opening up of the Russian Saps and digging communications between our own and the German system of trenches, making crossings for the artillery, repairs to roads to LOOS, assisting the Infantry to entrench on Hill 70, etc.

The 180th Coy R.E. assisted in the constructions of the Russian Saps and during the operations lent great assistance to the 74th Coy R.E. in the consolidation of the German system of trenches, in the repairs to roads, etc.

During the preparatory work and in the actual fighting the conduct and bravery of officers and men in the R.E. Companies was all that could be desired.

The 15th Signal Company, R.E., deserves the greatest credit for their share in the operations. It can, I think, be truly said that the communications throughout were maintained in a very efficient manner and this was entirely due to the unceasing and untiring efforts of all ranks in this unit.

(sd) G.S. CARTWRIGHT. Lt. Col. R.E.
C.R.E., 15th Division.

2/10/15.

Signals

Report on the system of communications of the 15ᵗʰ Div. in the operation near Loos and Hill 70 during the period 21.9.15 – 30.9.15

A H Mitchell
Capt RE
O.C. 15ᵗʰ Sig. Co. RE.

1/10/15.

Report on Communications during the fighting at LOOS and HILL 70 on 25.9.15 - 26.9.15.

1. PRELIMINARY MEASURES:-
The existing wires between MAZINGARBE, QUALITY STREET, LOOS ROAD KEEP and LENS ROAD KEEP were improved and fresh wires laid. The existing wire in the trenches were improved and replaced by new D5.

The arrangement of the wires is as shown in the attached diagram. (Fig 1)

Of the wires from Div. HQ to the HQ of brigades:-
 1 wire - an existing power wire - was buried 1 mtr. 50.
 2 were almost entirely in Trenches and the remainder were partly in trenches, partly laid across the open, behind rails in ditches or otherwise both ~~concealed from view and~~ protected from splinters & traffic and concealed from view.

The weather during the operations was wet and the ground sodden. The wires laid in the open and on the sides of tracks were in many places buried by the weight of heavy transport moving over and near them. No wires were cut by traffic but as a result of being so buried in wet ground it was found impossible to use a ringing telephone on these lines owing to leakage and on the morning of the 26th a "poled cable" line was laid between MAZIN GARBE and QUALITY STREET for use as a telephone line. With lines in the communication trenches little or no trouble was experienced. It was found that the best height to lay these was 18" above the bottom of the trench. i.e. knee high. Owing to the chalk in which the trenches were made "grooving" was not possible – as this process spoilt the side of the trench

The wire was "stapled" on the side of the trench and was held by "staples long" (obtained from RE field companies) at intervals of 10 feet, with smaller staples being used between these every 1' to 1'6" so as to keep the wire flat against the side of the trench.

Burying wires in the bottom of trenches was tried but was found useless as:-
(1) It was dug up by working parties improving the trench.
(2) In the rare cases where not destroyed as in (1) it became sodden and leaky.
(3) The labour involved in so burying the wire was excessive and not justified by the results obtained.

In addition to communication by wire provision was made to employ
(a) Visual
(b) Pigeons
(c) Wireless.

Fig. 2 shows the arrangements

made to link up Div HQ to FOSSE 3, QUALITY STREET and 4 visual stations in the trenches. It was proposed that visual stations should move forward with the attack but for various reasons very little use was made of visual.

ARTILLERY COMMUNICATIONS.

The GOC RA was linked up to the IV Corps RA, his own brigades and various brigades attached to him by lines laid by the Signal Company. A duplicate route was provided to each brigade. Ringing telephones to RA brigades were used as far as possible.
Wires were also laid to the Right and Left infantry brigades for use by RA observing officers with these brigades.
A detachment from the Signal Company under a subaltern officer (2nd Lt ERL Peake) were attached to RA HQ to lay & maintain these lines and control

traffic on them – This arrangement is considered a very satisfactory one –

All lines both for infantry & RA were manned during the bombardment which preceded the action and tested every ½ hour. There were test points at Div. HQ. LENS ROAD KEEP QUALITY STREET and MAZINGARBE CHATEAU.

The office at Div HQ was all prepared and instruments installed so that when the unit arrived at 6pm on 24.9.15 the operators sat down to their instruments and were able to work without further delay.

Work on 24.9.15.
Brigade HQ moved up on that day from MAZINGARBE CHATEAU and the House prepared at Div HQ to QUALITY STREET and LOOS ROAD KEEP respectively. The change took place smoothly both telegraphs

and telephone lines being in good order.

Work on 25.9.15.
The 45th Brigade HQ. arrived at LENS ROAD KEEP.
At 3 p.m. representatives of all three brigades were called on the phone, and checked their watches with an officer of the Div¹ Staff. Operation orders were issued over the wire to all brigades.

THE ATTACK.
Communication was kept up with the 44th brigade as follows.
QUALITY STREET was put in communication with a dug out in our N°6 trench which was used as an advanced report centre. From thence messages were sent on by runner or bicycle orderly to LOOS.
Wires were laid forward but frequently cut by shell fire.
An attempt to use the wire in the German trenches

was frustrated by a British officer who repeatedly cut the wire.

A line was got thro' finally to LOOS by the Brigade section but as it's existence was precarious a cable wagon was sent up about 3.45pm. and a DS line laid to LOOS which worked all thro' the night.

As regards the 46th Bde. When Bde HQ moved on to the HQ of the 7th KOSB wires were put thro' to that place.
2 Wires were run out during the attack and communication maintained by them with the battalions during the day. Runners were only used at intervals when these wires were broken.

The 45th Bde moved up to QUALITY STREET during the afternoon and used the 46th Bde Office to send and receive messages. Wires were laid by them to keep in touch with their battalions.

York on the 26th.

During the night 25th-26th The 45th Bde moved up to ~~Quality~~ LOOS and the 44th Bde back to QUALITY STREET.

It was considered desirable to connect LOOS to the Div. H.Q by means of a ringing phone. 2 cable wagons were sent out at 4.30 am on 26.9.15.

One laid a poled cable line from MAZIN GARBE to QUALITY Street and the other under Lieut. J.F. CHADWICK laid a line from QUALITY STREET TO LOOS. Speaking on these lines was excellent till about 9 am when the wires was cut and in spite of the effort of the linemen the shelling was such that neither this line nor the bnz -3 in line to LOOS could be kept "through".

The Signal officer at LOOS (Lt J.F. Ormsby) then made excellent use of the remain--ing means of communica--tion at his disposal viz:

(a) Pigeons
(b) Wireless.

Both these were singularly successful and by means of them the G.S. 15th Div. kept en fait with the situation at LOOS.
The wireless finally broke down owing to being discovered by a German "jamming" station which proceeded to drown all its signals.
Shortly after this the HQ 45th Bde was established at QUALITY STREET.
Dispatch runners from QUALITY STREET to LOOS were also employed to send messages to the 45th Bde.

MOTORCYCLISTS.
Owing to the bad state of the BETHUNE–LENS road E of QUALITY STREET the use of motorcyclists was well nigh impossible. 2 motorcyclists were sent to deliver messages to LOOS on the night 25th–26th. They left their bicycles at the top of the crest E of QUALITY

STREET and then proceeded to LOOS on foot.

Communication with neighbouring units.
Wires were used to connect the 15th Division to the 47th + 1st Divs. Motorcyclists to communicate with the 21st + 24th Divs.

GENERAL NOTES.
1. Ringing phones were much used in this action – the G.S. 15th Div. being connected up to the bri= gades as well as to the IV." Corps and neighbouring divisions (1st + 47th)

4.10.15

A H Turner Swift
Capt RE
O.C. 15th Sig. Co. RE

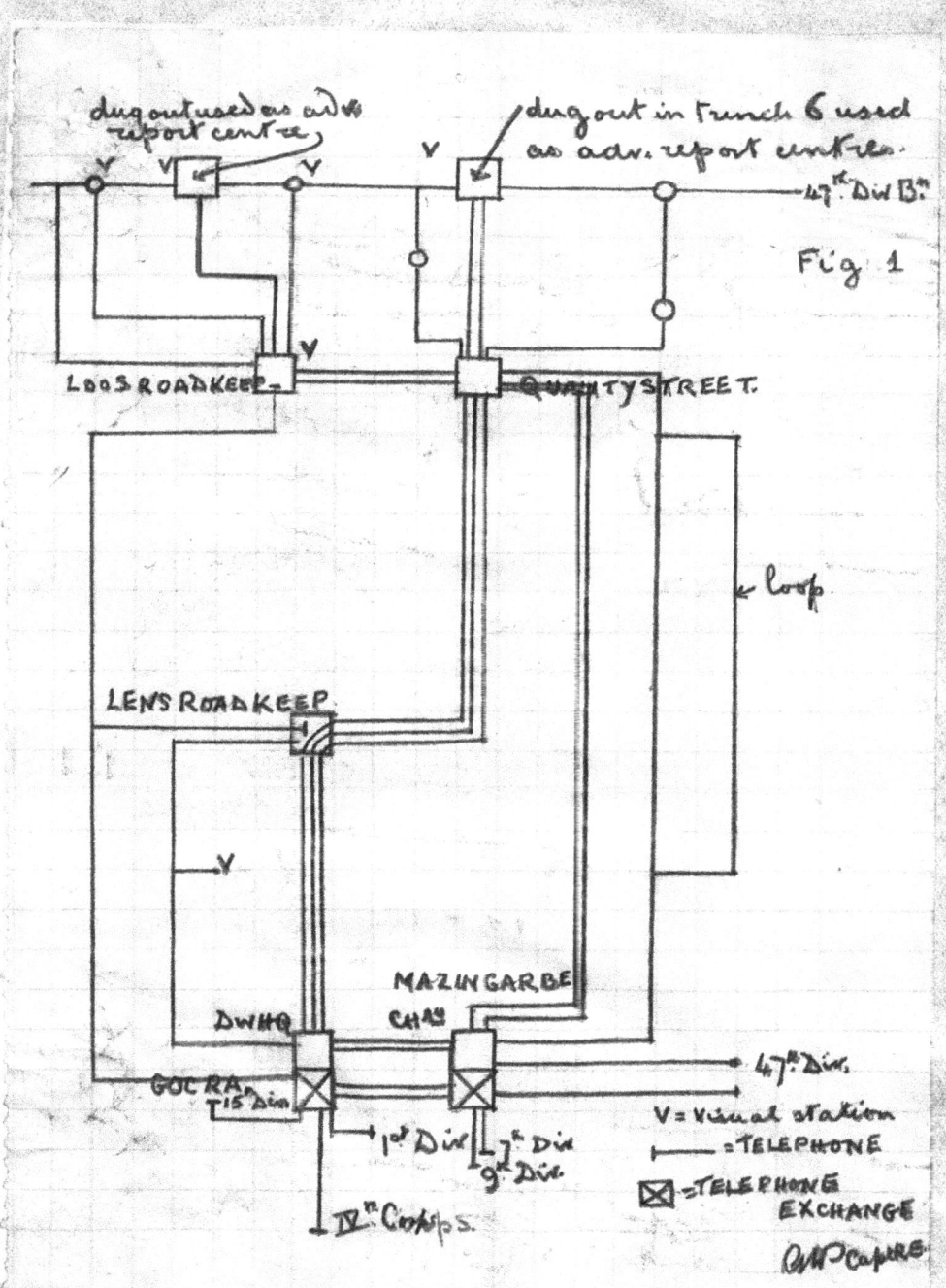

Arrangements for Visual Communi-
-cation.

Fig:-2

V_3 = Station in Support Trenches near telephone offices.

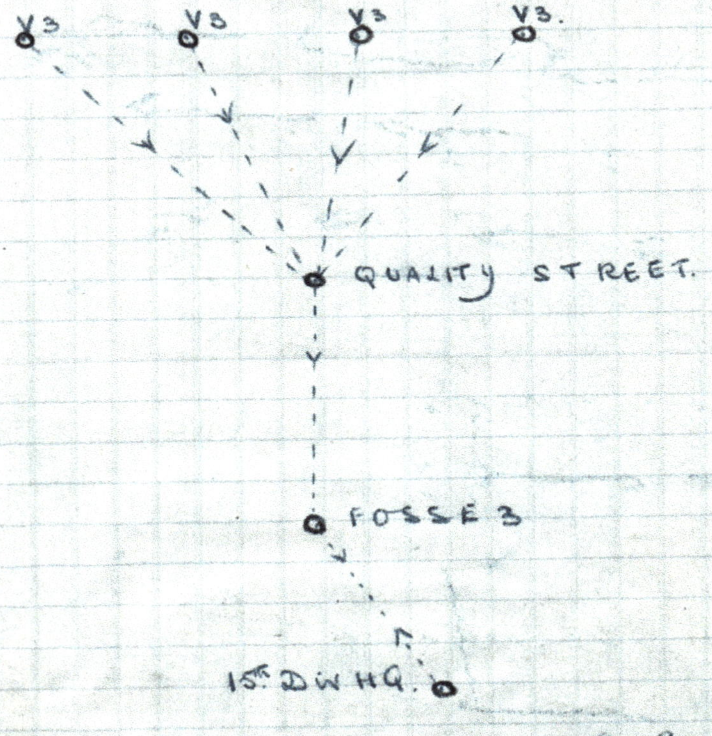
V3
V3
V3
V3.
QUALITY STREET.
FOSSE 3
15th DIV HQ.

→ Arrow shows direction of sending.

A.H. Thurlow

4. 11th MOTOR MACHINE GUN BATTERY.

Report from 11th Motor Machine Gun Battery - Operations
September 21st to 30th, 1915.

To O.C., Divisional Mounted Troops.

I beg to report as follows:-

1. September 21st to 23rd inclusive. Continued preparing dug-outs at the base allotted to this battery in L.17.b.4.4. (1/40,000. 36.b).

2. September 24th. Received orders to remove battery to above base. Started from VAUDRICOURT 8.10 p.m. arrived 8.35 p.m.

3. September 25th. Informed I was under direct orders of D.H.Q., but received through you, at 10.50 a.m., an order to report to 44th Infantry Brigade Headquarters. Started at 11.10 a.m., 4 officers, 54 O.R., 8 Solo Cycles, 19 Cycles with side cars, 4 box cars, 6 guns, 83,000 rounds S.A.A.

Arrived QUALITY STREET 11.20 a.m., G.O.C.44th Infantry Brigade was on the road. Halted battery for one minute only. Received verbal order "take your guns to LOOS and help support us on Hill 70, if you can get them there - the road is not yet bridged".

4. Progress along the LENS Road was fair until our second line trench. From there onwards the clay bogged the wheels and progress was very difficult. At each trench I waited until a party of the 74th Field Coy R.E. had bridged by filling in. I was forced to dismount my men and push and lift the cycles over the impossible places. I went forward and found the road beyond the German trenches in good condition and the LOOS Cemetery Road quite good.

5. It being now 12.30 p.m. I gave the order for the

/guns

guns to advance in the handcarts. This order was received after 5 sidecars had been pushed over 250 yards of mud, etc. So that the guns of Nos 1 and 2 Sections came on their cycles At the cemetery the road was crossed by a trench. We tried to bridge this with wooden tombstones, but it would not carry the cycles so I left them under fair cover by the road side. The guns went forward, being carried. No 3 Section quickly followed with guns in hand carts. No.2 was the reserve section but rushed on and I put No.1 in reserve at the cemetery trenches.

6. Capt Cooke, 15th Divisional Cyclists, met me at the junction of LENS and LOOS Roads, bearing instructions for me to report to 46th Infantry Brigade. He then proceeded promising the aid of some of his men to carry ammunition for my sections, as we were on foot. His detachment followed him 400 yards in rear. I warned these men and other supports to the side of the road as rifle fire down the road was lively Capt Cooke gave me very valuable aid in personally guiding one of my sections and some of my men, sent up later, to Hill 70.

7. The LENS Road was being shelled, 1.30 p.m., and I returned to my cycles and cars. With the assistance of the remaining men all the cycles and cars were moved back over the crest of the Hill and left on the side of the road, leaving the road quite clear for traffic.

8. At 5 p.m. I received a fifth box car.

9. No.3 Section with two guns reached a position on the North of the mine dump G.36.d.9.5. early in the afternoon and

/by

by 4.30 p.m. had dug themselves in. Royal Scots and some Camerons were in this trench. The 18th London Irish dug a support trench 150 yards in rear. It is a good trench. During the evening the East Yorks reinforced the front line.

September 26th. It was fairly quiet until 2 a.m. when fast fighting began and lasted through the dawn. My guns fired about 8,000 rounds each. During the British attack, beginning at 9 a.m., my guns kept up overhead fire, which proved effective. The Royal Scots charged successfully 3 times but received no support from the East Yorks.

At 3 p.m. my men being exhausted and the belts being wet and difficult to fill to prove effective, the Major i/c the trench ordered the section to evacuate, which it did, picking up the cycles at the cemetery and returning along the LENS Road, meeting a party with a box car which I had sent forward to find them.

10. 2nd Lt. C.O.D. Anderson commanding No.3 Section and I beg to call attention to his commendable services and very gallant conduct. By request he looked after other M.G's in the trench. He was also responsible for the barricades and guards on the mine dump which effectively stopped the enfilading. With the assistance of an officer of the 18th London, he stopped a stampede of the East Yorks. He started a communication trench between front and support lines but the fire was too intense. He brought his guns and men out safely under heavy fire and trying circumstances.

11. No. 2 Section got their guns in position on the N. of the sunken road early in the afternoon and dug in with the 10th Gordons and other troops. It was not a trench but a succession of small pits. Five Lewis guns were there also.

/By

By request, Lt. MacFarlane of my Battery looked after these guns. The left flank especially was being enfiladed and a trench was therefore dug 60 yards below the crest of the Hill and the line retired to it at 8 p.m. 25th. Rapid fire began at 2 a.m. and continued intermittently until 7 a.m. 26th. Late in the afternoon of 25th Capt Cooke guided some of my men with ammunition to No.2 Section. At 3 a.m. the Northumberland Fusiliers relieved the 10th Gordons. At 8 a.m. our artillery opened fire but for some time practically shelled our trench. The left of our line had, for a period, to evacuate. At 9 a.m. our line attacked. Major Hall, Northumberlands, ordered the machine guns to also advance. The Infantry returned hurriedly and the guns were with difficulty brought back. Major Hall, Northumberlands, was wounded in the first assault.

6 more assaults were attempted but the majority of the battalion did not participate. The ridge was carried several times but enough men could not be got up to hold it. It was in the fourth attack that Lt. Macfarlane was mortally wounded. He rallied the Northumberlands, stood on the parapet to encourage them and led them for 25 yards when he fell, one of my gunners and two cyclists carried him into the trench and later to the dressing station at LOOS. Serjt. E.N.G.White of No.2 Section took command/and was assisted by Serjt Scott and six cyclists in working the guns. The guns gave the infantry plenty of support. Serjt Scott, Cyclists, was also instrumental in rallying the Infantry and behaved most gallantly.

About 3 p.m. one of my guns was smashed by a bullet and shortly after the other jammed. The guns were ordered out of action and retired.

/12.

12.   Lieut. Macfarlane and Serjeant E.N.G.White. The work of this officer and N.C.O. are worthy of attention. They both behaved most gallantly, and Lt Macfarlane, if he had stayed by his gun, instead of so bravely helping the situation, might have been alive to-day.

13.   No.1 Section unfortunately lost its commander Capt B.Arthur on the afternoon of 25th. He was wounded in the thigh by shrapnel while sitting in a trench at LOOS Cemetery. He was taken safely back to the base and evacuated. O.C. Cyclists kindly lent me 2/Lt Duncan who had passed a Vickers course at the 15th Divl. M.G.School. He took charge of No.1 Section for me. This section was always in reserve in good machine gun positions with alternative positions ready.

14.   To bring safely the guns, men and M.T. out of action looked like a problem as a machine gun was playing on the Cemetery Road and the LENS Road was being shelled, however, it proved an easy, though extended matter. By making several trips with the box cars I was able to man the serviceable cycles and tow the damaged ones. A majority I got out in the early hours of the 27th. By 9 a.m. 27th I had all my men (excepting casualties) and all M.T. excepting one Douglas Solo, which was borrowed by a 1st Divisional Despatch Rider and has not been returned.

14.   Battery Serjeant Major David M.Herd rendered valuable assistance and behaved most gallantly under the trying circumstances of extricating men and M.T. He also assisted me splendidly during the night 25/26 when an endeavour was made to straighten out the transport tangle at the LENS ROAD Redoubt.

/15.

15.   Casualties - Lieut. Macfarlane killed, Captain Arthur and 1 O.R. wounded. 2 O.R. were slightly wounded but continued on duty. 6 men were gassed by the gas shells on morning of 26th due to them not having their smoke helmets ready for instant service. They recovered in a few hours. The box covers of three cars were struck by bullets and shrapnel but the damage is practically nil. 11 bicycles and side cars were hit by shrapnel. Three were so badly damaged that on the 27th I loaded them into the box cars and sent them to repair shop at AUCHEL. The others were repaired by my own fitters, who also repaired the one gun damaged.

16.   Communication I found good except that at times it was very difficult to find the H.Q. desired or a working telephone. Communication was kept up with my section throughout the night 25/26 by men from my battery on foot. No.3 Section, after retiring to support trench, was out of touch and not returning to the rendezvous for some time, was reported missing. My searching party eventually met the section on the LENS Road.

17.   A feature of our work was the usefulness of the hand carts, which the G.O.C. allowed me to have made. These were also used in taking ammunition to Hill 70 for the 44th Infantry Brigade.

18.   September 27th. Entire battery occupied in cleaning and repairing.

19.   September 28th. Stood by ready to move at one hour notice as per orders received at midnight 27/28. At noon received orders to move to DROUVIN. Started 12.45 p.m., arrived 1.10 p.m. Remained in billets.

/20.

20.   September 29th.   Received orders to move to LABUISSIERE, started 4 p.m., arrived 4.30.

21.   September 30th.   At billets in LABUISSIERE refitting.

22.   The enemy troops at Hill 70 were 22nd Regiment, 157th or 153rd and 233rd. The latter shoulder strap had a grenade on it and probably was artillery.

23.   There was practically no road control.

24.   A sketch map is attached roughly showing my gun positions on Hill 70.

2/10/15.   (sd) C.B.HALL. Major.

Sketch — Not To Scale

Enemy Working Party
Crest 250-300 yds
HILL 70

Lewis Guns 44 rds
× MG Battery Guns

Fire Trench
Later 44 Batt Infantry ×
Northumberland Fus × M Gunners killed
Fus

Sp't 151 yds

Sunken Road

200 yds
11 A.S. M.M.G
2 guns
4 PM 25th
Till 10 AM 26th

× 13th London

M.M.G at
11 AM 25th
Till 2 PM 26th

Spt Line

Lot of E York's
Stopped here to
dig. Left at
Fire Trench

Railroad Line
Barricade 5 Men
Guard 5 Men

Mine Dump

Double Pylon

Lewis Guns of E. York's
brought in late in the evening
of 25th

LOOS

5. 15th DIVISIONAL CYCLIST COMPANY.

15th Divisional Cyclist Coy.

Report on Action 25th 26th and 27th Sept

1. **Distribution of Company**
On 24th September the Company was distributed as follows —
In dugouts in MAZINGARBE — Headqrs and 3 Platoons and 1 Officer and 1 Section of another Platoon.
On Control Posts 2 Platoons (less 1 Officer and 1 Section)
Escort to Prisoners 1 Platoon.

2. **First Orders to move** on 25th
At about 11.45 a.m. received orders to send two Platoons to LOOS & for the Commander to report to Adv. Div H.Q. for instructions. I therefore reported in person to Divl H.Q. & was ordered to report to G.O.C. 46th Inf Bde and to instruct the O.C. 11th M.M.G. Batty to do the same. As exact position of H.Q. 46th Inf Bde was not known, I was instructed to go to the Church in LOOS where an orderly would meet me with further orders. However on reaching the church the

orderly was to be found & the vicinity was being very heavily shelled.

3. <u>Progress of the ~~Company~~ Detachment to LOOS</u>

On passing through QUALITY STREET was told by an officer that we were urgently required so pushed on as quickly as possible.
At the German front line trenches the mud on the LENS road was so bad that cycles had to be carried. This delayed matters. The 11th MMG Batty were likewise affected. I found O.C Batty & told him we were both to report to GOC 46th Inf. Bde. After reforming my leading Platoon we pushed on & soon after turning off the LENS road came under rifle fire. I increased the pace & got under cover of a wall in the outskirts of LOOS. Two men were hit & the rear had to take cover from shell fire.
Only a small party arrived in LOOS with me.

4. **Advance through LOOS**

Shortly after arrival in LOOS No 2 Section ~~under Lieut~~ 11th MMG Batty under Lieut McFarland came up carrying their guns & some ammunition. I therefore left one of my officers 2nd Lieut Duncan to reform my detachment told off all the men with me to help ~~with~~ carry guns etc for No 2 Sect MMG Bty & advanced through LOOS. Lieut McFarlane went on to reconnoitre & I verified position by map. Having arrived at the situation I sent ~~a~~ them on & ~~party & got~~ the party with two guns got established in the front line on HILL 70.

I went back to bring up the remainder of my detachment & also collected some odd men of No 2 Section MMG Bty who had a hand cart with ammunition. We went forward through LOOS & I halted the party under a bank 100ˣ in rear of the support line & went on to reconnoitre & ascertain the situation.

5. Reconnaissance on HILL 70

On reaching the firing line about the centre of the hill I found that all units of the Division were mixed up. I reported to several Commanding Officers but could not find one of the 46th Bde. As our lines on the hill were crowded with men, I consulted O.C 7th Camerons as to advisability of withdrawing my detachment after ascertaining what the situation was on the left.

I went along our line to the left discussing the situation with officers en route & finally reached the LA BASSEE – LENS road about 400ˣ South of PUITS 14 BIS. where I found a detachment of about 100 7ᵗʰ R Scots Fus This flank appeared to be rather in the air & was being shelled by our own guns. I wrote a message to O.C 7th Camerons explaining the situation & took it back part of the way myself.

Then returned to my detachment left a squad under Sgt Scott to assist No 2 Sec. MMG Batty – sent an officer's patrol under 2nd Lieut Duncan by a less exposed route further over to the left to join touch with the 2nd Bde; ordered one platoon under 2" Lieut Chubb to withdraw to a communication trench near LOOS CEMETERY & went back myself to report.

6. LOOS

Met G.S.O 2 of 15th Div explained what I knew of situation. He wrote message which was despatched in duplicate by 4 of 2nd Lt. Chubb's Platoon back to DIVl H.Q.
Received no further orders but was instructed to remain in LOOS. Distribution of Cyclist Detachment was then as follows —
2nd Lt Chubb's Platoon more or less complete in communication trench near LOOS cemetery.
2nd Lt Duncan out with a patrol to left of 15th Div. One Squad of his Platoon on HILL 70 with N°2 Sec MMG Batty; another with N°1 Sec MMG Batty in trench near LOOS cemetery. The remainder with me as orderlies. I attached myself to H.Q 44th Bde

and later to 45th Bde when G.O.C 45th Bde took over the line & endeavoured to assist with guides and messengers.

At about 9pm or more a number of messengers etc were constantly being required. I got 2nd Lt Chubb's Platoon established in a cellar in LOOS. 2nd Lt Duncan reported that he had got into touch with 2nd Sup Bde on our left & had explained how our line was situated. As the officer i/c No 1 Sec MMG Batty had been wounded I ordered him to take over command of the Section.

Later, ammunition was required by firing line on HILL 70 & 2nd Lt Chubb with his platoon made numerous trips throughout the night & early morning of the next day 26th.

The situation remained the same until early in the afternoon. My detachment got still further split up owing to a party of 2nd Lt Chubb's Platoon who got separated being ordered by a Medical Officer to act as stretcher bearers & I decided to withdraw & reform. 2nd Lieut Duncan brought out No 1 Sect. M.M.G Battery from the trench that was being heavily shelled & succeeded in bringing them back under heavy fire.

7. Behind the line
I reported to Divl H.Q about 4pm on 26th for further orders & was instructed to reform & collect as many men of the Company as possible and report to G O C 46th Inf Bde at LOOS ROAD keep taking up all stragglers with me.
I was ordered by G O C 46th Inf Bde to halt near QUALITY STREET on the morning of 27th I handed over the stragglers which I had collected & later about 11.30pm received orders to withdraw to billets in MAZINGARBE.

8. Recommendations
I would like to bring to your notice the names of the following officers and N.C.O —
2nd Lieut R.N. CHUBB who made numerous journeys through LOOS under heavy artillery fire taking

up ammunition to the firing line on HILL 70.

2nd Lieut T. M. DUNCAN who successfully carried out a reconnaissance & got in touch with 2nd Inf Bde under fire, & later took command of No 1 Sect MMG Batty.

No 1585 Sjt F SCOTT who greatly assisted No 2 Sec MMG Batty on HILL 70, remaining there until both guns were disabled.

J C Cooke Capt
Cmdg 15th Divl Cyclist Coy

1.10.15

6. 15th DIVISIONAL MOUNTED TROOPS.

Report on Operations Sep 24-28.
15th Divl Mounted Troops

Sep 24. 7pm Squadron moved up to NOEUX les MINES & bivouaced there

3 platoons cyclists & MMG battery to dug outs prepared behind MAZINGARBE. O/C Mtd Troops with them. Remainder of cyclists under A.P.M.

Sep 25 10.30 a.m. Orders received for 11th MMG Battery to proceed to QUALITY STREET to report to 44 Infy Bde. They are to be moved forward later to Northern outskirts of LOOS at discretion of GOC 44 Infy Bde with a view to support our attack on Hill 70.

In answer to further enquiries they are instructed to take no cyclists with them & to leave F. Trench mortar battery at MAZINGARBE.

They started off at 11-10. The O/C 11th MMG Battery reports their further progress.

11.45 Orders received for Two platoons of cyclists to get ready & for O/C cyclists to report to Divl HQS.

They started off about midday. O/C cyclists reports their further progress.

11.50. Orders received for squadron to move up to join me at MAZINGARBE.

They arrived at 1.30 having been much hindered on roads full of cavalry & supporting troops.

Report on Operations Sep 26-28.   Sheet 2.

12.0 midday. Thousands of cavalry pass between NOYELLES & MAZINGARBE. Continuous stream for more than an hour.

21st Division begin to arrive from NOEUX les MINES & form up in L.16 b & L 16 c just behind our position & halt there.

Squadron complete + one platoon of cyclists st and by
12 midnight   for orders for remainder of day.   (LOOS
Trench mortar was ordered to report to 46 Inf Bde

Sep 26. 11.30 a.m Remaining platoon of cyclists sent for to assist battle police.

12 midday. One troop of cavalry ordered to report to APM for escort & road control work. Despatched No 1 Troop at 12.15. They remained out till 6 p.m Sept 27th.

4 p.m. Orders received that remainder of squadron is to go out & work under 44th Inf Bde dismounted. Rode up to Fosse 7 & sent back horses from there. Report to 44th Inf Bde in QUALITY STREET at 5.15 p.m. with 57 men.

6.15 p.m. Carry entrenching tools to O/C 7th Camerons + 10th Gordons. Take up 100 picks + 100 shovels in two journeys to original German trenches at our LENS road.

Report on Operation Sept 24-28.   Sheet 3.

8 p.m. Carry rations to Bde Headquarters and send party with rations to 10th Gordons in old German trenches near LENS road.

10 p.m. Unload a lorry of smoke helmets at RE Stores Quality Street.

Midnight. CRE asks for 20 men to assist in repairing LENS road send troop up under 2 Lt Burns Lindow.

Sep 27 2.30 a.m. Orders received at Bde HQS that the Division is to come out to billets in MAZINGARBE. Marched back to dugouts at L17c arriving there at 4 a.m.

9 a.m. Find MMG battery has returned during our absence. O/C Cyclist Co with two platoons returns during the morning.

6 pm. No 1 Troop return from APM also platoon of cyclists.

10 p.m. Sent for to Divl HQS. & receive orders to be ready to move at 1 hours notice with all available Mounted Troops. Order cancelled at 9.30 a.m Sep 29. & Mtd Troop ordered to march to billets at DROUVIN.

Sep 28.

J W Cooper Major
O/C 15th Divl Mtd Troops.

Report on Operations Sept 26-28.   Sheet 4.

Sep 27. 12.30 a.m. Ordered to send out two officers patrols
to find position of captured German field
guns in LOOS.

2nd Lts Robinson & Barns Linton went out
but found themselves in the middle of the
Guards Division who were advancing
towards LOOS & were unable to make progress
before dark. They returned not having
discovered the guns, having been held up
by the heavy bombardment directed against
the Guards Division till the light gave out.

They were instructed to be ready to start
again at dawn but the orders were subsequently
cancelled.

7. "F" TRENCH MORTAR BATTERY.

Report on Operations Sep. 24-28

F. Trench Mortar Battery.

Sep 24	Moved up to dug outs near MAZINGARBE with 11th M.M.G. Battery.
Sep 25/6	Midnight. Received orders to proceed to LOOS & report to 46 Infy Bde HQs
Sep 26	3.30 a.m. Arrived LOOS with Mortars & ammunition proceeding by motor lorry to QUALITY STREET & thence man handling guns & ammunition forward.
	Could not get in touch with 46 Infy Bde HQs which had been moved. Found 62 Infy Bde who had no orders for me.
	No opportunity offered for use of mortars, so assisted in removal of wounded till midday Sep 27.
Sep 27	Received information that 46 Infy Bde was at LOOS ROAD KEEP. Returned there & reported.
	Waited for orders till 2.30 a.m Sep 28 when ordered to return to billets in MAZINGARBE, bringing out mortars & leaving stores of ammunition at LOOS — ~~LOOSR~~ QUALITY KEEP NORTH and QUALITY STREET.

C.A.Elliot Lieut.

8. 44th INFANTRY BRIGADE.

Report on attack on 25th September 1915

On the 21st September 1915 a bombardment of the enemy's trenches opposite 15th Division front commenced.

At that time my Brigade was disposed as follows:-
In X.1. Front system   10th Gordon Highlanders.
In Grenay-Vermelles main trenches   8th Seaforth Highlanders
In billets + dugouts in Mazingarbe. 9th Black Watch.
In billets at Verquin -   7th Cameron Highlanders.

The bombardment continued from 21st to 24th September. On the 22nd September the 7th Cameron Highlanders moved from Verquin about 7p.m. + occupied the Grenay-Vermelles branch line of trenches arriving about 11 p.m.

The casualties during this period were
10th Gordon Highlanders O.R.   10 killed   33 wounded.
8th Seaforth Highlanders O.R.   1 wounded
7 Cameron Highlanders O.R.   3   "
         Total   10 killed 37 wounded -

2. On the night of 24/25 Sept the Brigade moved into position in the forward Trench lines for the assault -

At 4pm. on 24th the Brigade H.Qrs. moved from Mazingarbe Chateau to Advanced Report Centre in Quality Street -

3. At 2am. 26th Sept. reports from all units were received that they were successfully in position for the assault -

These included reports from 73rd Field Coy. R.E. and G Company 9th Gordon Highlanders (Pioneers) who were attached to the Brigade -

Night was fine. Wind slightly W. of South –

4. At 3 am. hour of zero was reported as 5.50 am.
Watches had been synchronized at 5 pm 24th inst.
At 5.50 am. gas & smoke discharge commenced –
Wind not very favourable & too light causing inconvenience to occupants of front trench –

5. At 6.30 am. the assault was launched –
The Brigade moving as follows. –
In two columns each on a front of two platoons
The 9th Black Watch on the R. with Right flank on the LENS ROAD –
The 8th Seaforth High'rs on the L. with flank resting on Boyau 8C –
The 7th Cameron High'rs were in support
The 10th Gordon High'rs in Brigade Reserve
I sent one section R.E. & one platoon 9th Gordon High'rs in rear of each assaulting column –
The 7th Cameron High'rs were ordered to support at such a distance as would ensure their being able to re-inforce when & where required –
The 10th Gordon High'rs in Brigade Reserve were ordered as soon as the assaulting columns & supports were clear of the German first line trenches to occupy them & with the assistance of the remaining 2 sections R.E & 2 platoons 9th Gordon High'rs (Pioneers) to open up communication trenches from our front line to the German front line & await orders –
At the moment of the assault 2 companies of

3

the 10th Gordon Highlanders occupied our trenches from SAP 18 to the LENS ROAD — together with their 4 machine guns + the 4 machine guns of the 9th Gordon High". (Pioneers), two of which were to be in SAP 18 so as to bring an enfilade + covering fire on the LENS ROAD REDOUBT —

All the other machine guns moved with their Battalions under orders of the Comm'g Officers —

The guns of the 9th + 10th Gordon Highlanders were under the Brigade Machine Gun officer as a Brigade Reserve —

6. The assault was well carried out, the two leading Battalions going with great dash over the parapet at the enemy's trenches —

The LENS ROAD REDOUBT was strongly held by machine guns — + the casualties were heavy at first especially in the Black Watch who faced the Redoubt —

The defence was quickly worn down + at 7.10 am the columns were reported as over the German second line trench —

At 7.45 am I received a report that the 8' Seaforths were approaching LOOS which they could see through smoke and mist —

7. The German 3rd line gave little resistance, but some wire in front had to be cut, which caused a little delay + a few casualties as machine gun fire was opened from some houses N.W. of

LOOS about G.29.d.1.2.

8. At 8.5 am. the advanced part of the Brigade was reported as in the outskirts of LOOS. The Seaforths on the N + Black Watch towards the S.

A regular street to street + house to house fight then took place - bombing parties doing excellent work in houses and cellars - but the enemy did not make any regular stand as they were kept well on the run + the bayonet was freely used -

Some very gallant actions were reported of bombers, who attacked any house from which fire was opened -

A number of Germans surrendered - They seem to have been taken entirely by surprise, as they mostly had no equipment on + everything was left in confusion -

By this time the units had got considerably mixed + the 7th Camerons had mostly joined with the other two Battalions -

9. At about 7.45 am. I ordered the 10th Gordon High'rs in Brigade Reserve to move from the German trenches + support the main attack of the Brigade leaving it to the C.O. Officer to use his own discretion as to where he could best assist the attack, but at the same time to watch the right flank in case of any attempt to counter-attack from the direction of LENS -

5

10. At 8.45 a.m. a report was received from the Black Watch & Camerons that the advanced troops had passed through LOOS.

The enemy were still on the run & offering little opposition.

11. At 9.25 a.m. a message was received from the O/C 10th Gordon Highrs that he was pushing on with the whole Battalion through LOOS as the Camerons were still ahead.

12. From reports received HILL 70 was occupied without serious opposition by the 44th Brigade about 8.30 a.m. as a report sent off at 8.55 a.m. by O/C 7th Camerons states machine guns of 9th Gordons had gone up to the hill with those of 10th Gordons.

No official confirmation of the HILL being occupied was however received until later when it came from 2 or 3 sources.

13. During the fighting through LOOS there was a tendency for the left of the attack to swing round towards the S. pivotting on the Right flank.

This was partly due to the conformation of the ground but principally I think from a natural tendency to follow prominent features such as the PYLONS at LOOS and the CRASSIER. So that by the time the Brigade had reached HILL 70 the front line was facing S.E.

14. Reports were received about that time that the front of the attack was being held up by heavy rifle & machine gun fire from CITÉ

ST AUGUSTE, but on comparing this on the map, with the officers who sent reports, there appears no doubt that it should have read CITÉ ST LAURENT and the salient at the DYNAMATIÈRE which was full of machine guns.

This fire forced those who had proceeded over the Hill to retire as it was found impossible to advance in face of such opposition & the casualties were numerous — & eventually a position was taken up with the Carrier as the right about G.36.d.3.5 running through a natural bank about H.31.c.6.9 to H.31.b.2.7 —

The German work at H.31 central was not occupied by the enemy on the arrival of the first line —

15. All the Battalions of the Brigade were now mixed up about 10 a.m. & also some 7th R. Scots Fusiliers & some of the 46th Brigade —

Colonel Sandilands who was on this part of the Hill took over command of all the mixed parties near him & commenced digging in & consolidating the position —

It was unfortunate that through the over-keenness a number of the Brigade had pushed on so far over Hill 70, as it caused a great many casualties, who could not be got back —

16. Two reports, one sent at 10.15 a.m. & one evidently later but without hour from Capt. C.S. Tuke were received by me at 11.25 a.m. stating his position

the line. This officer was Brigade Machine Gun officer & had gone forward with the 8 guns of the Brigade Reserve viz 4 each of 9th Gdns & 10th Gdns —

I received no further report from him & I regret that he is still missing & I can get no account of where he was seen last —

17 At 10.15 am I ordered my Brigade Signal officer to go forward & establish communication with LOOS. So that I might advance my H.Qrs. He had already carried his line forward to the German trenches —

This he proceeded to do, but I could not get into communication with him, as it appeared afterwards his line was continually cut —

18 At 10.40 am I received a message from 15th Divn that the Motor Machine Gun Battery had been ordered to report at my H.Qrs.

They arrived shortly afterwards & I gave the officer Comdg instructions to proceed to the N. outskirts of LOOS & assist the forward line — This he did & the Battery afterwards did extremely good work at HILL 70 & suffered several casualties —

19 At 11.10 am I received messages that reinforcements were required, which I sent on to the Division —

I believe the 45th Bde were then either on their way to reinforce or moved directly afterwards —

Ammunition was also asked for & as much as possible was sent forward & I have received no report that at any time the supply failed —

8

At 1.30pm - 4 machine gun limbers (1 per Batt^n) with pack saddles & ammunition under Lieut Holmes of Seaforth High^rs were sent forward to LOOS. or as far as they could get & to do what was possible in getting S.A.A. up to the HILL -

I also ordered the Brigade Tool carts to be horsed & sent forward as soon as it was safe to do so, as the men had very few tools beyond the entrenching tools they carried -

Owing to great congestion of traffic on the LENS ROAD they did not get down to LOOS till past midnight -

20/ At 3pm I moved to LOOS with my Brigade Major & most of my staff as I had established communication through, leaving my Staff Captain at Quality Street till I arrived -

On arrival at LOOS however I found the wires had been constantly cut & the place under the PYLONS at first chosen was being heavily shelled so moved to a house near at G.35.b.2.2. where I found the O.C. 7th R.Scots Fusiliers - He was endeavouring to establish telephone communication but his wires were constantly out of order -

Communications was consequently to a great extent lost & only kept up to a limited extent by runners from units to Quality Street -

21/ At about 5pm a Batt^n of East Yorkshire

9

Regt arrived belonging to the 62nd Brigade which I had been told was coming up to relieve my Brigade —

I met the Comm'g Officer who asked me the way to HILL 70 — & I showed him, pointing out to him which side of the PYLONS to keep.. He informed me the remaining Batt'ns of the 62nd Brigade were also just arriving —

He then went forward, but apparently joined with the 142nd Brigade on our Right —

I saw no other troops of the 62nd Brigade & I tried to find the Brigadier as I was told he was in LOOS, but could not get hold of him —

22 About 7.45pm Colonel Sandilands 7/Camerons & Capt. Straug 8/Seaforth came to my temporary H.Qrs & discussed the situation with Major Wace representing 15th Division —

It was decided to place Col Maclean 13th R. Scots in command of the troops on the HILL & for him to see how much he could relieve the remains of my Brigade —

Colonel Maclean then left with Col. Sandilands & my Brigade Major, Major Rainsford Hannay for HILL 70 —

23 I remained until my Brigade Major reported to me that Col. Maclean had consolidated the position & had arranged for the Seaforths and Camerons to be relieved at once — & that they were proceeding on their way back into reserve —

10

Major Hannay remained until the other two Battalions were relieved & then rejoined me in Quality Street —

Brig. Genl Wallerstein commg 45th Infy Bde had arrived at the same HQrs during the time these arrangements were being carried out — & I left him there on my return —

24. On my way back I found troops lining some of the German 3rd line Trenches & was told they were another Yorkshire Battn. of the 62nd Brigade —

I did not see any Northumberland Fusiliers —
On arriving at the main LENS ROAD I found it terribly congested with transport — mostly first line — cookers &c — it was impossible to move carts anywhere —

The next morning a lot of it was destroyed as well as animals by the enemy's shells —

I don't know how it got there —
I had only ordered my Brigade Tool Carts & some water carts to go down under cover of darkness & to return before daylight —

My tool carts were handed over to the 45th Brigade, but it was impossible to get them back —

I have since sent for them, but those most of the tools were there on the 28th; the waggons were smashed —

25. By 6 a.m. 26th Sept — what remained of my Brigade were back in the GRENAY —

VERMELLES Line of Trenches –

I then got an order to move them to our original
first line trenches + later they were ordered to the
German trenches which they occupied at dusk –
+ were established there when I went round later
in the evening + were in touch with the 8th K.O.S.B.
on their left –

26 During the day a great many stragglers belonging
to various regiments were returning along the
LENS ROAD towards Quality Street in rather
disorder –

I got some officers of my Bde + 46th Bde + some
police + stopped as many as we could –

I collected various officers + put them in charge
+ eventually sent about 400 to man the front
British trenches N. of the LENS ROAD –

They consisted of Yorkshire Regts, Northumberland
Fusiliers (2 Battns), Somerset Light Infy + others –

Later I got a large number of Lincoln Regt +
Durham Lt Infy + odd lots, placed them under
officers + sent them to the front line British Trenches
S. of the LENS ROAD when my own Brigade
moved into the German trenches –

There were several members of some Divisional
Staff arrived during that day, but they did not
take any steps to collect the men –

The Brigadier + Brigade Major of the 62nd Brigade
were at my HdQrs in Quality Street during part
of the day –

27. About 1.30 a.m. 27th Sept an order was received for the 44th Brigade to move into billets at Mazingarbe —

This order was carried out & they arrived in Mazingarbe between 3 a.m. & 5 a.m. & went into billets under arrangements made by the Staff Captain.

I went with my H.Qrs for that night to Chateau Annand, but moved in the morning later to Mazingarbe Chateau —

I attach a list of casualties as far as can be made out —

Since the 27th Sept several parties of men have turned up —

One party of 1 N.C.O. & 10 men of 9th Black Watch had got detached from their Battn when going through LOOS on 25th Sept & joined a Battn of the 47th Division on our Right —

They remained with this Battn under a Capt Wilkinson until the afternoon of 28th when they returned when relieved, staying the night at Le Brebis & reporting here the next day —

28. In conclusion I should like to speak of the splendid behaviour of all ranks —

Though a stream of wounded was returning all day on the 25th there were no sound men returning with them.

The slightly wounded cases were helping those who could not get on by themselves —

13

The very large proportion were making their own way, even badly wounded cases —

One man of the Camerons was wounded in the hand with another wound in the head he had on his back a comrade who was shot through the leg —

All were cheery — no grumbling or complaining. Many went after their wounds were dressed by foot to Noeux-les-Mines rather than take up room in ambulances which were required for more severe cases —

Several after being dressed both officers & men returned to the firing line & remained till relieved —

Where all did so well it would be invidious to make distinctions & it is difficult to say which had the most right to be proudest, the officers of their men or the men of their officers.

The young officers proved themselves most devoted to their duty, sticking to their work often after being wounded.

The 73rd Field Company. R.E and G Company 9th Gordon Highlanders must be included in the excellent work of the Brigade —

Both suffered heavy casualties in officers & men — List of recommendations for good service has been forwarded separately.

2 Oct 1915.

14

Casualties 25th 26th & 27th Sept
44th Infantry Brigade

9th Black Watch
OFFICERS

KILLED
- Maj. M.W. Henderson
- Captain J.M. Ball
- Capt. D.M. Graham
- Lieut. J. Crighton
- " J.C. Henderson-Hamilton
- 2nd " A. Sharp
- " " J. Millar

Died of wounds: Capt & Adjt R.E. Harvey
Missing (believed killed) Capt. C.S. Tuke
  Brigade Machine Gun Officer

WOUNDED
- Capt. A.K. McLeod
- Lieut R. Andrew
- " A.C. Dennistoun
- " E.R. Wilson
- 2nd " D.J. Glenny
- " " J. Campbell
- " " R. Stirling
- " " G. Scott-Pearson
- " " W.J. Leslie
- " " F.R. Wilson
- Capt F.A. Bearn R.A.M.C.

Wounded & missing —
Lieut J.H. Cameron

Other Ranks Killed 168 Wounded 319 Missing 192 Total 679

8th Seaforth Highlanders
OFFICERS

KILLED
- Major A.J.N. Tremearne
- Capt. A.G. Ravenhill
- Lieut A. Miller
- " J.Y. Stanford
- 2nd " G.M. Calder

Missing
- Lieut J.E. Kennedy
- 2nd " F.L. McCrae
- 2nd " W.C. Tremearne
- 2nd " G. MacGregor

WOUNDED
- Lieut. Colonel N.A. Thomson
- Major V.P. Swinburne
- Capt. H.F. Munro
- " R.M. Powell
- Lieut. D.B. Macaulay
- " D.M. Dunlop
- 2nd " A.W. Turnbull
- 2nd " J.R.S. Payne
- 2nd " J.M.L. Nicholson
- 2nd " W. Heath

Other Ranks — Killed 144 Wounded 362 Missing 194
Total 700

Casualties (continued).   15

10th Gordon Highlanders

OFFICERS

KILLED - nil
WOUNDED & MISSING -

WOUNDED

Major C. Maitland-Makgill-Crichton -   Lieut R. L. Watson
Lieut R. O. Christison -   2" " G. W. Syme
                                         2" " G. J. Lumsden
                                         2" " L. G. Robertson
                                         Lieut A. R. Roche R.A.M.C.

Other Ranks - Killed 23 Wounded 221 Missing 114. Total 358.

7th Cameron Highlanders.

OFFICERS.

KILLED

2nd Lieut D. A. Stuart
"   "   E. G. Taylor
"   "   S. McDonald
"   "   B. Watt.

MISSING.

Capt. W. H. Kirkland -
 "   P. K. Cameron
2nd Lieut S. E. Chapman.

WOUNDED

Capt. N. McLeod
 "   L. R. Douglas-Hamilton
 "   G. A. C. Davy
Lieut W. G. S. Stuart
2nd " A. McNiven

WOUNDED & MISSING

Major J. Barron -

Other Ranks
        Killed 134 Wounded 255 Missing 115. Total 534

73rd Field Coy R.E.   KILLED
                        2 officers -   15 O. Ranks.
                      WOUNDED
                        3 officers -   33 O.R "

G. Coy. 9th Gordon Highrs   KILLED
                              2 officers
                            WOUNDED   } 71 O. Ranks -
                              2 officers

9. 45th INFANTRY BRIGADE.

45th Brigade - 15th Division.

Report on Operations from 21st September to the
30th September, both dates inclusive.

21-9-15. 13th Royal Scots)
) in billets at NOEUX LES MINES.
          11th A & S Hrs.   )

          Bde Hd. Qrs.   )
)
          7th R.Scots Fus.) in billets at LABUISSIERE.
)
          6th Cameron Hrs.)

22-9-15. As above.

23-9-15. 3 p.m. Bde Headquarters moved to NOEUX LES MINES.

5.30 p.m. 6th Camerons moved to billets and bivouac at DROUVIN.

5.50 p.m. 7th R.Scots Fus. moved to billets and bivouac at VAUDRICOURT.

24-9-15. 8.30 p.m. Bde Headquarters moved to advanced Headquarters in LENS Road Redoubt.
Battalions of the Brigade marched to MAZINGARBE into positions of readiness.

25-9-15. The Brigade complete was in position of readiness at 1.55 a.m. cookers and water carts were with their battalions until shortly before dawn when they rejoined the remainder of the 1st Line Transport at the walled in triangle south of MAZINGARBE CHATEAU; the horses of these cookers and water carts only remaining with their vehicles. All other animals being sent to NOEUX LES MINES.

At 5.50 a.m. . 40 minutes discharge of gas interspersed with smoke from candles was delivered after which the assault by the 44th and 46th Infantry Brigades was launched punctually at 6.30 a.m. The 45th Infantry Brigade in touch with the two leading Brigades, commenced moving forward until 9.30 a.m. when it occupied the positions in our front line system of trenches, two battalions in each of the areas occupied by the 44th and 46th Infantry Brigades respectively. Owing to the receipt of an order, said to have been passed from the Brigade reserve of the 46th Infantry Brigade on their left, the 7th R.Scots Fusrs (less their battalion Headquarter

followed /

followed the 44th Infantry Brigade through LOOS to HILL 70, where they are reported to have materially assisted in the retention of the western slope of the hill.

At 10.35 a.m. the grenadiers of the 6th Camerons were put under the orders of the G.O.C. 46th Infantry Brigade and proceeded to bomb northwards along the German front line trench from SOUTHERN GAP towards LONE TREE in order to assist the 2nd Infantry Brigade held up opposite that front. This bombing party progressed for 60 or 70 yards but were stopped by a strong barrier manned by hostile bombers with a machine gun.

At 11.30 a.m. the 6th Camerons, under orders received from the 15th Division, were sent forward with their right directed on PUITS 14 bis to support the left of the 46th Infantry Brigade and with orders to place themselves under the command of the G.O.C. 46th Infantry Brigade.

At the same time the 7th R.Scots Fus. were ordered to move forward into the German third line trenches between LOOS Cemetery and G.29.c.3.9 when it was discovered that they had already moved forward. They were at once sent an order not to proceed further forward than HILL 70 and were to place themselves under the orders of the G.O.C. 44th Infantry Brigade. The 11th A & S H being ordered, instead, to man the German third line trench west of LOOS.

At 11.45 a.m. the 13th R.Scots were sent forward to hold the German front line trench from LENS Road Redoubt to LOOS Road Redoubt.

At 12.40 p.m. the 13th R.Scots and 11th A & S Hrs were ordered forward into LOOS and to hold it in order it release troops of the 44th and 46th Infantry Brigades and to be ready to reinforce either of those Brigades, if called upon by them to do so. At this hour Brigade H.Q. moved forward to QUALITY STREET and there found 44th Infantry

Brigade /

Brigade Headquarters.

At 3.10 p.m. news was received that the 62nd Infantry Bde. had been ordered to move on LOOS, and, if HILL 70 was still held by our troops, to, if necessary, relieve them.

At 3.30 p.m. the leading battalion of the 62nd Brigade passed through QUALITY STREET.

News from the 13th R.Scots and 11th A.& S. Hrs now became scarce and nothing definite was discovered until Major Wace, G.S. 15th Division arrived from LOOS and explained the situation.

The 13th R.Scots and 3 companies of the 11th A. & S.H. had been called upon to support the leading brigades on HILL 70 and the 45th Infantry Brigade was now to relieve such parts of 44th and 46th Infantry Brigades as the situation would admit. Major Wace had seen Lt.Col.McClear, D.S.O. 13th R. Scots and placed 3 companies of 13th R.Scots, 7th R.Scots Fusiliers and 3 companies 11th A.&.S.H. under him with orders that he was to consolidate the position.

At 8 p.m. Brigade Headquarters moved forward to LOOS and relieved the G.O.C. 44th Infantry Brigade. It was ascertained that the troops on HILL 70 were much mixed up but owing to the situation a re-grouping was not possible. Tools were got forward and ammunition and the companies proceeded to improve the trenches they had already dug with what available tools they had carried and with their entrenching implements. The enemy's artillery was active throughout the evening and night, their fire being directed on the troops holding the slope of HILL 70, upon LOOS village and upon the LENS Road.

26-9-15. At 12.30 a.m. the enemy delivered a counter attack on the 7th R.Scots Fus:, the right hand battalion of the Brigade. The attack was easily repulsed our machine guns being greatly aided by a large fire from the enemy's rear in the direction of LENS which showed up the attackers very distinctly.

At 5 a.m. /

At 5 a.m. orders were received to attack in conjunction with the 62nd Infantry Brigade THE REDOUBT on the North East end of HILL 70 and to occupy the hill, to cover an attack by 21st and 24th Divisions.

The Battalions being much scattered the task of organising them for the attack was difficult in addition to which the enemy delivered, at about 5.30 a.m., a heavy counter attack from a South-easterly direction.

The G.O.C. 62nd Inf.Bde. and O.C.Battns were consulted and the attack was arranged to take place at 9 a.m., after an hours intense bombardment by all available guns.

7th R.Scots Fus.on the right, 11th A. & S.H. in the centre, 13th R.Scots on the left closely supported by three battalions of the 62nd Infantry Brigade.

As the right hand battalion was to keep touch with the 47th Division throughout and it was feared this battalion would be drawn in towards the REDOUBT thereby causing a gap, assistance was asked for and a battalion of the 47th Infantry Brigade was ordered to cooperate and cover the right flank of the attack.

The forward troops, ordered to be drawn back to a safe distance during the bombardment could not be withdrawn before 8 a.m., for fear that the enemy might advance and occupy the trenches left vacant, but were successfully retired a short distance immediately the guns opened.

The bombardment was extremely accurate in spite of the difficulties to observation caused by a mist, though a certain number of shells fell on our front line.

At 9 a.m. punctually whistles were blown and the front line went forward.

The enemy's fire was heavy, particularly that which enfiladed the Hill from the direction of the S.E.corner of the DOUBLE CRASSIER. The left and centre of the assaulting line came under our own artillery fire and the attack failed, though

supports /

supports were brought forward and another charge was attempted.

The supporting brigade, it is stated, never came on, though had it done so it seems extremely probable that the position would have been carried. One officer, since killed, who succeeded in reaching the outer defences of the REDOUBT, stated that he saw the defenders running away back.

At 11.10 a.m. two battalions, which have not yet been clearly identified retired hurriedly from the neighbourhood of PUITS 14 Bis leaving our left flank exposed. One of these battalions was however rallied and once more took up its position in the line. During this time the Brigade was shelled and was under rifle and machine gun fire all of which caused heavy casualties.

Reinforcements were asked for and it was pointed out that with their left flank exposed the battalions would find difficulty in maintaining their position.

A message was received that reinforcements were arriving. One battalion to LOOS and another battalion from NORTH MAROC- both of the 47th Division - but these battalions were not seen.

At 12 noon a fresh Brigade commenced an attack against the enemy's trenches in front of CITE ST AUGUSTE but never developed and failed to progress.

On being heavily shelled the attack completely collapsed and with no apparent signs of any attempts to rally, the troops returned rapidly to the German 1st Line trenches. The failure of this attack and arrival of reports that the Germans were advancing as if to outflank our left made the position appear most precarious, reinforcements were asked for and it was pointed out that unless the recent attack was reformed the Brigade would be unable to retain its position.

Parts of the line held by the brigade now began to suffer

further /

further losses and to fall back until a message was received that they were now holding the lower slopes of HILL 70. on the outskirts of LOOS, where they were told to hold on. Ammunition supply became difficult over the open, men were not available to carry it up from the Brigade Reserve and sufficient men to carry it could not be withdrawn from the firing line.

At 1.5 p.m. an order was issued to battalions that if forced to retire they were to do so on the German front line trenches between LOOS ROAD and LENS ROAD REDOUBTS. The line on the western slopes of HILL 70 was held until between 4 and 4.30 p.m. when through some mis-interpretation of the above order those portions of regiments that could be collected were withdrawn to LOOS just at the time that the village was entered by the 6th Cavalry Brigade. Parts of the Brigade remained under the orders of the G.O.C. 6th Cav.Bde and assisted in holding the village until late that night when they were relieved and withdrew to the VERMELLES BRANCH of the GRENAY Line.

Throughout the 25th and 26th the intercommunication between battalions and the Bde. and between the Bde. and the Division was remarkable. At times the wires from LOOS to QUALITY ST. were out but messages were got through by both carrier pigeons and short range wireless – the latter however being "jammed" after the third message had been sent.

27-9-15.	The brigade was billeted in MAZINGARBE.
28-9-15.	The brigade marched to billets in HAILLICOURT.
29-9-15.	The brigade marched to LABUISSIERE, halted for the day and in the afternoon 3 battalions moved to billets in BRUAY.
30-9-15.	The 3 battalions at BRUAY returned to LABUISSIERE and bivouaced.

Sd. F.E.WALLERSTEIN. Br.General.
1-10-15.   Commanding 45th Infantry Brigade.

10.   46th INFANTRY BRIGADE & UNITS.

        (A)   10/Scottish Rifles.
        (B)   7/K.O.S.B.
        (C)   12/H.L.I.
        (D)   12/H.L.I.
        (E)   8/K.O.S.B.
        (F)   91/Field Co. & "H" Co. 9/Gordons.
        (G)   91/Field Co.
        (K)   91/Field Co.

REPORT of 46th INFANTRY BRIGADE on OPERATIONS between
21st and 30th September.

September 21st.

1. On September 21st the Artillery commenced their first day's bombardment; confining their attention principally to efforts to cut the German wire entanglements, their shooting was very accurate and considerable damage was done to the German wire and also to the LOOS ROAD REDOUBT. There was practically no retaliation on the enemy's part.

The situation of the Brigade this day was as follows:-

7th Bn K.O.Sco.Bord.	PHILOSOPHE & MAZINGARBE.
8th Bn K.O.Sco.Bord.	LABEUVRIERE.
10th Bn Scottish Rifles.	MAZINGARBE.
12th Bn High. L.I.	Occupying the front system of trenches in Sector X.2 and part of X.1 with Headquarters at QUALITY STREET.

The wind caused considerable anxiety by remaining in the East, and officers in the front system were detailed to take meteorological observations at 4., 4.30 and 5 a.m. each day.

September 22nd.

2. The bombardment continued throughout the night and during this day.

The practice made by the Gunners still remained excellent and by this evening the wire was practically sufficiently cut to enable an attack to succeed. No effort was made to cut the wire on the North side of LOOS ROAD Redoubt. There was still but little effort to reply on the part of the German artillery. During the night of 21st/22nd, and, in fact, during each night of the bombardment, heavy rifle and machine gun fire was maintained on the German lines to prevent working parties mending their wire.

/Situation

Situation of Brigade:-

7th Bn K.O.Sco. Bord.	All in PHILOSOPHE.
8th Bn K.O.Sco. Bord.	Half Battn MAZINGARBE.
	- do - SAILLY line of defences.
10th Bn Scottish Rifles.	MAZINGARBE.
12th Bn. High. L. I.	Holding front system.

Patrols were sent out to examine the wire and reported that there was a certain amount of low wire which required cutting.

September 23rd. 3. Third day of bombardment. Artillery still continued directing its attention to German wire to make certain of it being efficiently cut. It also, of course, fired on the enemy trenches.

At 3.55 p.m. an intense bombardment of the enemy trenches took place, lasting for five minutes. At the end of this time the infantry opened rapid fire and also machine gun fire. Then the Artillery again fired on the hostile trenches. The object was to make the Germans believe an attack was going to take place and so get them to man their trenches when it was hoped the resumption of Artillery fire would kill some of them. They only, however, replied with a few rifle shots but a good many shells were fired into our lines, four men being wounded.

Situation this night:-

7th Bn K.O.Sco. Bord.	One company in front system of trench, 3 companies - PHILOSOPHE.
8th Bn K.O.Sco. Bord.	As on 22nd.
10th Bn Scottish Rifles.	One company in front system of trench, 3 companies in MAZINGARBE.
12th Bn High. L.I.	One company in MAZINGARBE.
	" " " PHILOSOPHE.
	Two companies in front system.

/Patrols

Patrols again went out. Those in front of right Company reported wire sufficiently cut - those in front of left companies could not get near enough to see on account of hostile fire.

Our own wire was cut to allow passage of troops.

24th September. 4. Bombardment of hostile trenches and wire continued. Especially vigorous during night 24th/25th to prevent enemy mending wire.

Whole brigade moved into forming up area. The day being cloudy this movement commenced about 4.30 p.m., the whole movement was completed by 11 p.m.

By this hour 11 p.m., every battalion was in its area and arrangements made for giving the men breakfast before starting next morning.

Brigade Headquarters moved to LOOS ROAD KEEP.

25th September.
26th September. 5. See separate report.

27th September. 6. During night 26th/27th the remnants of the brigade moved to MAZINGARBE, it reached here early in the morning and went into billets there.

Throughout the day efforts were made to collect stragglers, and clean up the men. In the afternoon burial parties were sent out.

28th September. 7. Brigade marched to billets at HAILLICOURT. Every effort being made to replace lost kit and equipment.

29th September. 8. Brigade remained in same billets which are insufficient for its needs. During day reinforcements of some 200 men altogether for Brigade arrived.

Classes of working machine gun commenced.

30th September. 9. Brigade received orders to evacuate all billets South of BARLIN - LABUISSIERE Road. This necessitated one battalion bivouacing.

Steady drill and rifle exercises by all battalions.

The attached general account of the operations on
September 25th and 26th, 1915., is
forwarded together with:-

A. Report from 10th Bn. Scottish Rifles, as to action
of No.3 Column.

B. Report from 7th Bn K.O.Scottish Borderers, as to
the action of No.4 Column.

C. Report from Colonel PURVIS as to the action of No.5
Column. Owing to all the officers of this column
having become casualties, this report is not complete.

D. Report from Lt. Colonel PURVIS, 12th Bn. H.L.I.
showing the part played by the 12th Bn H.L.I. (less
two companies).

E. Report from Lt. Col. SELLAR, 8th Bn. K.O.Scottish
Borderers, as to action of reserve.

F. Report from Major POLLARD-LOWSLEY as to the part
played by 91st Field Company and "H" Company 9th
Gordons.

G. Report from Capt. SAYER, R.E., showing the events of
Hill 70 on the morning of 26th September.

K. Further report from O.C., 91st Field Company R.E.,
(manuscript).

OPERATIONS 25th/26th.

Reference trench map Sheet 56.c. N.W.

1. The morning of September 25th, 1915, broke dull and cloudy with a very gentle wind blowing from between S.S.W. and S.W. At about 5.15 a.m. the wind, from the same direction, increased in strength, but only slightly. Inwardly everyone was wondering whether the wind was sufficiently strong, and from the right quarters, to justify the discharge of gas. At 5.50 a.m., however, these misgivings were quietened, though not actually dispelled, by seeing the discharge commencing. Everyone was then asking "Is it going in the right direction?" There was evident relief when it was seen to be doing so - but slowly, the wind was hardly favourable for this discharge.

From the Brigade Headquarters at LOOS ROAD KEEP the sight of the gas and smoke clouds as they rolled towards the German lines was magnificient; but everything beyond this white and yellow cloud was invisible. A few moments after the discharge began, heavy rifle fire commenced to be poured into our trenches. The German shell fire, however, was not so severe as was anticipated. It was distinctly noticeable how the hostile rifle fire gradually decreased in volume as the fumes reached the German lines; its intensity, however, was only diminished; it never ceased altogether. At 6.15 a.m. the 12th Bn. H.L.I. reported one gas cylinder had burst and that two were leaking badly.

2. Immediately previous to the commencement of the assault Piper LAIDLAW, 7th Bn. K.O.Scottish Borderers, jumped up on to our front parapet and piped away, though gas fumes surrounded him, and heavy rifle fire was sweeping our trenches.

Exactly at 6.30 a.m. the troops crossed the parapet and made for the German lines. As a matter of fact they would have suffered less if they had waited another five minutes or so owing to the slowness with which the gas was travelling; the

/order

order, however, was 6.30 a.m. and so the troops left at that hour; but a considerable number were gassed.

The German wire was crossed without much difficulty, the Artillery having cut it thoroughly. Heavy casualties, however, were suffered between our lines and the German trenches, which shows that the gas was not so efficient as supposed. In fact from what could be seen, and from what others state, it seems to have done more harm to our own troops than to the enemy.

3. No.5 Column suffered heavy losses in crossing into the German trenches, these losses were due:-

(a) To the supposed "Southern Sap" proving to be no sap at all; hence the bombers told off to bomb along it were severely handled. The fact that no sap existed is interesting because the aeroplane photographs distinctly showed a trench there - in reality it was a mere scrape in the ground.

(b) The 2nd Infantry Brigade on our left, not getting on as quickly as was anticipated and so this column suffered severely from rifle fire from their left.

4. By 7.5 a.m. the whole of Nos 3 and 4 Columns had reached the German front system and immediately pushed on. The whole of No.5 Column (less two platoons) were also across by this hour. From this moment the advance was continued steadily by Nos 3 and 4 Columns without much opposition, except shell fire past LOOS, entry into which seemed to be easily avoided by the attacking troops, in spite of several machine guns enfilading our line as they advanced. This, however, may be accounted for by the rapid progress made by the 44th Infantry Brigade through this village.

5. The 2nd Infantry Brigade on our left is stated to have suffered severely from the effects of gas and also to have found the German wire uncut. This resulted in it being completely stopped, and not until well into the afternoon could it get forward and then only, it is understood, by the assistance of another Brigade which was sent to attack these

/German

German trenches from the North east.

Meanwhile our attack progressed rapidly far more so than evidently had been anticipated; but owing to the situation of the 2nd Brigade, the safety of our left flank caused great anxiety. It was on this account also that the situation of No.5 Column was rrendered the more difficult. This Column had large casualties on reaching the German front trenches, especially amongst bombers on account of no trench being found in the Southern Sap, and, therefore, it had not the men available to bomb towards the 1st Division. It could only maintain itself in the trenches won with difficulty, losing nine out of ten officers killed and wounded, and more than half its men. Captain Torrance, however, managed to hold on until assistance was sent him in the shape of some 100 bombers of the 6th Cameron Highlanders, and, in addition, one platoon of the same regiment as a covering party.

6. The exposure of our flank had an appreciable effect on the operations. Our troops knowing that the 2nd Brigade should be on their left were continually sending out patrols to look for it. When no trace of it could be found messages were sent back to the Division asking for troops to be sent up at once to protect our left. This resulted in the 6th Camerons being sent up with their right directed on PUITS No.14 Bis. Not only did the rapidity of the attack lead to the exposure of our left flank, but also it placed in serious jeopardy the whole of the assaulting column since no provision had been made to pour in the continual flow of reinforcements so necessary for the success of such an operation. After some time, the remainder of the 45th Infantry Brigade was sent on but this was like a mere drop in the ocean and would have been better if another Division could have been following up close at hand ready to push throught the leading Division when that one was exhausted.

The attack started at 6.30 a.m. and instead of a fresh Division being ready to advance at - say 10 a.m., as should

/have

have been the case for a successful termination to the operations, no sign of its arrival was seen until nightfall. If, therefore, the whole of the 45th Infantry Brigade had been pushed in at 10 a.m. there would have been no support for the Divisional Commander to fall back upon in case of a reverse, for some 8 - 10 hours.

7. Our assaulting columns reached the line Hill 70 - PUITS 14 Bis Chalk Pit at about 9 a.m. after suffering considerably whilst getting into the German front line. So easily was Hill 70 captured, however, and so much were the Germans on the run, that the attacking troops could not unfortunately be stopped. This led to their undoing. South of the Hill 70 are the houses belonging to the outskirts of LENS. These had all been placed in a state of defence. They bristled with M.G's and, in addition the Germans rushed M.G's up to the Railway embankment just North of the houses. The troops, exhausted as they were by their vigorous attack and without artillery support, could not face it, and had to withdraw to Hill 70 where they were ordered to consolidate. Here for the remainder of the day attack and counter-attack for its possession continued. It was during this withdrawal that the Brigade suffered heavy casualties.

8. About one hour before dusk, General Matheson went forward with the object of seeing the position at PUITS 14 Bis, but on approaching Chalk Pit Wood he saw the PUITS being heavily shelled so changed direction on to the Chalk Pit. As he did this he met Colonel SELLAR, 8th Bn. K.O.Scottish Borderers who explained the situation on the left to him. General Matheson then went on to Chalk Pit where he met G.O.C. 2nd Brigade and arranged details for night defence, i.e., that 2nd Brigade would be responsible for PUITS No. 14 Bis inclusive.

9. At the end of the day the crest of Hill 70 and the work on top of it was in the hands of the Germans.

/Our

Our troops were digging themselves in just below the crest. The troops holding this line were a mixture of 44th, 45th and 46th Infantry Brigades. Later on in the night the 44th Infantry Brigade was withdrawn. The line held at nightfall was from just below the crest of Hill 70, with a portion of the work in our hands, to PUITS 14 Bis, at which point we were in touch with the 2nd Brigade. Our troops in the work on Hill 70 as well as those below the crest were heavily shelled by our own artillery. At about 7 p.m. General Matheson visited G.O.C. 44th Infantry Brigade in LOOS and met their Major Wace G.S., 15th Division. The Brigade Advanced Headquarters were in a German trench at G.29.b.3.2. Communication with the Division from here was impossible, all four wires which had been laid out being cut. Afterwards it was discovered they were cut by our own troops who had orders to cut all lines in the German trenches. At about 9 p.m., therefore, General Matheson decided to go back to his Headquarters at LOOS OAD KEEP, where he was better able to get touch with the Division and get out the necessary orders. He left a representative at his Advanced Headquarters. By this time it had been raining heavily for several hours, and all the telephone instruments had got thoroughly soaked rendering them useless. During the night orders were received that PUITS No. 14 Bis would be taken over by the 21st and 24th Divisions, who were responsible for the line from here to the North, while the 46th Infantry Brigade was told it would be relieved by one battalion of the 62nd Infantry Brigade.

10. No communication was received from Headquarters, 62nd Infantry Brigade, as to which battalion was to come under Brigadier-General Matheson's orders. Even the position of the 62nd Brigade Headquarters was not discovered for some time. This was eventually discovered through the 15th Division, and a copy of the order for the battalion which was to relieve the troops of the 46th Infantry Brigade was sent to the 62nd Infantry Brigade Headquarters.

/The

The latter sent this copy on to the Battalion - 13th Northumberland Fusiliers - and the latter received it some time during the night; but there is nothing to show they received some amendments and additions to this order issued later.

Meanwhile during the night Lt. Col. Purvis, Commanding 18th Bn. H.L.I., who had come to Advanced Brigade Headquarters to see General Matheson, and who had been told that a battalion of the 62nd Infantry Brigade would relieve the troops of the 46th Infantry Brigade, found that battalion wandering about looking for 46th Infantry Brigade Advanced Headquarters. Knowing the orders, Lt. Col. Purvis took charge of this battalion, and himself placed it in the position it was to get into during the night. Having done this, Colonel Purvis returned to Brigade Headquarters at LOOS ROAD KEEP and reported his action.

11. At 9 a.m. the 62nd Infantry Brigade was to have attacked Hill 70, the 46th Infantry Brigade remaining in support. This attack was to be preceded by one hour's intense bombardment.

Between 7.50 and 8 a.m. on 26th, General Matheson arrived at his Advanced Headquarters. On arrival, parties of men of the 46th Infantry Brigade were seen coming back from Hill 70. These parties were stopped and ~~asked~~ asked where they were going, they replied that they had been relieved and were told to go back. By this time most of the officers had become casualties, and none was to be seen with these retiring parties. General Matheson, therefore, went forward to the bottom of Hill 70 and stopped all men coming back, placing them in position along the LOOS - BENIFONTAINE Road.

Captain Sayer, 91st Field Company, R.E., was then sent up to stop any more men coming back and place them in the same place, and, generally, to take charge of them. From this position they were well placed to support the attack of 62nd Infantry Brigade on Hill 70.

12. This attack commenced at 9 a.m. and at first seemed to go

/without

without a hitch. Troops poured up Hill 70 and over the crest to the South-west of the work. Most of the work itself was still held by the Germans, but our bombers started working their way through it. The attack between Hill 70 and PUITS 14 Bis did not progress to the same extent, it appeared to suffer considerably from machine gun fire from the direction of PUITS 14 Bis and the Chateau South of it. An attack made between the Chalk Pit Wood and PUITS 14 was stopped by machine gun fire which seemed to come from a red house between this wood and the PUITS. To the North of Chalk Pit Wood, British troops were seen to be wandering aimlessly about, first going forward, then coming back again, going forward a little way and eventually running away. Almost at the same time the troops, who had crossed Hill 70, were seen retiring, some stopped for a few minutes where the remnants of the 45th and 46th Infantry Brigades were digging themselves in just below the crest; but others still kept retiring and eventually the whole, except a very small portion of these 21st Divisional Troops, were in retirement. The handful of men of the 15th Division on Hill 70 rallied the troops of the 21st Division several times but at last the latter were incapable of being rallied any more and went, leaving the remnants of 15th Division with a few remaining men of 62nd Infantry Brigade to hold Hill 70 alone.

13. Beyond a couple of German counter-attacks which were repulsed, there was no reason, apparently, for the panic produced in the 21st Divisional Troops. Certainly the Germans were using asphyxiating shells all that morning, and their artillery fire increased in intensity as if reinforcements of artillery had been received, but beyond this there seemed no cause for panic, except possibly from the fear engendered by machine gun fire. An unrestricted view of the whole front from Hill 70 to Chalk Pit Wood could be obtained from Brigade Advanced Headquarters, and watching this front most carefully through powerful glasses, no sign, except possibly for some dozen men on the

/skyline

skyline, could be seen of any Germans. Nevertheless, the whole battle front was covered with line upon line of men withdrawing. These lines came down Hill 70, swept up past Advanced Brigade Headquarters, back over the original German trenches, over our former/system, and on towards PHILOSOPHE.

Many attempts were made by General Matheson and other officers to check this tide, but all in vain, with the exception of a few men of the 15th Division who somehow had got mixed up in it and who at once obeyed the orders given to them. No attempt was made by any ~~other~~ of these troops to stand.

The men seemed incapable of grasping what was said. Ordered to get into trenches and reform, the men merely stared vacantly into one's face and walked on. They appeared bereft of comprehension and yet not a sign of a German was seen.

Realising the situation, General Matheson, about 10.30 a.m. sent a Staff Officer to report to Divisional Headquarters. About 11.30 a.m. as the flow still continued without check, General Matheson, himself, went back to LOOS ROAD KEEP to report the circumstances personally over the telephone to the Division. The Divisional Commander ordered him to Headquarters to report verbally; arriving there about 12.30 he received the G.O.C's instructions to get into touch with the G.O.C. 44th Infantry Brigade and with the remnants of the two brigades, and any men of 21st Division it was found possible to stop, to hold our original front line trenches. Meanwhile two cavalry regiments had been sent up into LOOS to hold that village and support the 15th Divisional troops still on Hill 70.

Arriving at QUALITY STREET, the Brigadiers 44th and 46th Infantry Brigades conferred and decided to hold the original frontage of their respective attacks, i.e., the 46th Infantry Brigade from 8 (c) inclusive to the North.

Leaving QUALITY STREET, General Matheson then went to ~~arrange~~

/arrange

arrange for this occupation, and still met men streaming back. A few of them he managed to stop and got them into our front line trenches. These trenches were full of gas fumes, so the men were allowed to lie down outside. Having organised the defence of this system, General Matheson then went over the German front line trenches where he met the remnants of Capt Terrance's party 12th Bn. H.L.I., with some 6th Cameron Highlanders.

He asked for volunteers to go and assist the remnants of the Brigade on Hill 70, and the whole of this party at once volunteered and went. This was the party that arrived on Hill 70 as the remnants were retiring from it about 5 p.m., and whose arrival helped our men to get back on to the Hill. Still there was no sign of any Germans except their shells, and still the flow of men to the rear continued.

14. In the meantime arrangements were made for feeding and watering our men, and as many of the 21st Division as possible. The one cry of the latter troops seemed to be that they were hungry and thirsty. Our own men, of course, were naturally hungry and thirsty also. Arrangements had been made on the afternoon of the 25th to get the cookers of each battalion to QUALITY STREET in the hope that it might have been possible to get some food to the firing line. Beyond some of the H.L.I., however, it does not seem that any of our other battalions got food. The cookers, however, were in continual use from the moment of their arrival making hot water for the wounded and feeding various stragglers who came in. Their presence helped the situation on the afternoon of 26th and enabled food to be sent up at once to the men holding our front trenches. It was not long, therefore, before all these men were fed. Water was also obtained for these men, there was some difficulty in obtaining it on account of the supply in QUALITY STREET running dry, but it was obtained from LENS ROAD REDOUBT, and carried up to the men in petrol tins.

/15.

15. About 6 p.m. the order came that a Cavalry Brigade was going to hold North LOOS Avenue where it would get into touch with the 1st Division until the arrival of the Guards Division; the 15th Division was to hold the German front system. On receipt of this order our troops, with a number of 21st Divisional Troops, were taken forward and placed in position in the German trenches, the 46th Infantry Brigade and 44th Infantry Brigade dividing the frontage between LOOS Road and the Southern Salient between them.

The Guards Division came up about 7 p.m. and prolonged the line to our left, the Scots Guards being next to the 46th Infantry Brigade and the Irish Guards immediately North of them. In the meantime the O.C. Somerset Yeomanry came in and asked for orders. He was told that presumably he and his dismounted men were to connect along North LOOS Avenue between LOOS and 1st Division, but that he was not under our orders in any way. He tried to telephone to the Cavalry Division but without much success. In the middle of the night he took his men away but where to is unknown.

Orders were received about 12 midnight to withdraw all men of 15th Division under cover of darkness to MAZINGARBE where they would reform, leaving the Cavalry and Guards to hold the position won. Brigadier-General Campbell, commanding Cavalry in Loos, being responsible for withdrawing the 15th Divisional remnants on Hill 70.

16. The remnants of the 15th Division had continued to hold their position on Hill 70 throughout the 26th September, repulsing several counter-attacks on the part of the Germans and rallying time after time the withdrawing troops of 21st Division. This remnant had suffered severely from the fire of men of the 21st Division who at one time were in positions behind them. About 5 p.m. they seemed to have withdrawn from the Hill on an order given by some one in the 45th Infantry Brigade; but at

/the

the bottom of the Hill they met some more troops coming up, 100 men, a mixed force of H.L.I. and Cameron Highlanders who General Matheson had sent forward.

On meeting these men the whole then returned to their original position on the Hill and remained there until relieved by the 3rd Cavalry Brigade about 12 m.n. 26th instant.

On relief, the remnant of the Brigade marched back to MAZINGARBE where they spent the night of 27th and collected their stragglers, etc.

17. The battle on 25th had not long been in progress before the problem of ammunition supply arose. Thanks, however, to the provision of Depots made beforehand, there was never any actual shortage of ammunition, but there was considerable difficulty in obtaining men, in requisite numbers, to carry the ammunition from QUALITY STREET to the Depots in the trenches and from these up to the firing line.

But the difficulty as regards getting ammunition from QUALITY STREET to the Depots in the trenches was overcome by getting up the pack ponies and carrying it on these. The parties organised in the first instance for getting ammunition from the trench depots to the firing line was soon used up, and as the battalion progressed it took a long time for the men to get from the depots to the firing line and back. However, by collecting all available men, the supply was kept up somehow, as, however, there seemed danger of the troops on Hill 70 running short of ammunition, messages were sent ordering up the S.A.A. carts and these were sent forward to LOOS. They suffered a number of casualties from shell fire, chiefly, however, amongst the animals. The troops in the 46th Infantry Brigade seemed to have been kept well supplied with ammunition, and therefore little use was made of these carts by them; but the presence of these carts was justified by the use made of them by the 44th

/and

and 45th Brigades and some troops of 21st Division. The total casualties from sending these forward was 20 animals killed, 14 wounded as well as two carts broken up.

18. The arrangements made for collecting the wounded left much to be dsired. The regimental aid posts were established in our front trenches. Advanced Dressing Stations were in QUALITY STREET. The regimental stretcher bearers collected wounded and took them to the regimental aid posts, from here the stretcher bearers took them on to the advanced dressing station. On arrival at the latter, if the case was serious the man was left on the stretcher for fear of hurting him if moved. This resulted, in a short while, in no stretchers being available for the bearers and this led to many of the wounded being left out and it is feared led to the death of many of them.

20. No mention is made here of the many gallant acts that were performed both by officers and men which helped so materially to gain the success achieved. It is presumed that these will all be recorded in the historical records of the Battalions.

This brief summary of the operations cannot however be closed without some slight testimony to the extraordinary fighting spirit displayed by all ranks. Every single officer and man was doing his utmost and nothing would have stopped them getting through. This is a fact well worth recording when it is remembered that about one year ago the profession of arms was foreign to most of these men.

Nothing could have surpassed the dash and fury with which the 12th Bn H.L.I., 7th Bn. K.O.Scottish Borderers, and 10th Bn. Scottish Rifles captured the German front system of trenches.

A   No 3 Column
10th Scottish Rifles

ATTACK ON HILL 70.   25/9/15.   PART 1.

1. Gas discharge at 5.50 a.m.

2. First two platoons mounted parapet and advanced at 6.30 ; the other platoons following in quick succession.

3. Between our 1st Line and German 1st Line our troops suffered heavily from Shrapnel, M.G. and Rifle fire.

4. Very few Germans in their 1st line trench, very little bayonet work done; German support line held by fair number. Germans retired in haste into LOOS.

5. The advance towards Hill 70 between LOOS Rd and N. LOOS Avenue was under very heavy German shrapnel fire and rifle fire, the latter coming from LOOS.

6. Troops made rapid progress between BENIFONTAINE - LOOS Road and lower slopes of Hill 70. On reaching slopes of Hill 70 troops were exposed to heavy fire from M.G's firing from vicinity of PUITS 14 bis.

7. Troops advanced up Hill 70 taking cover behind natural terraces; on reaching last terrace our troops were held up. Time 10 a.m.

8. Heavy rifle fire and M.G. fire from both sides lasting for 2½ hours. During this time the German fire increased gradually which gave the impression that reinforcements were being brought up. Ammunition appeared to be getting scarce and word was passed down to the right. About 12.30 p.m. our men began to give way, the number of wounded

being very great. Wounded streamed down hill in direction of LOOS; the line weakening gradually. The whole line retreated 50 yds or thereby where it again made a stand, meanwhile reinforcements from 45th Brigade came up. About 2.30 p.m. the original line was regained. The troops dug themselves in still further where they remained until dusk.

9. It was decided that troops should take up position along support line on 2nd terrace. Front line fell back on support line about 9 p.m. (time uncertain).

10. During the earlier part of the night we were greatly hampered by snipers in trees H. 25.d.38 and a battery located at M.6.d.7.8.. The latter endeavouring to enfilade us. Shells, however, landed about 200 yds west in vicinity of road running from Puits No 15 to Puits 14 bis. This was reported by wire and later battery appeared to be put out of action. On night 25/26th battery in chalk pit H. 25.a.7.5. very active firing on LOOS Tower and vicinity.

28/9/15

In the Field

(Sgd) James A. Callen, Lt.
10. SCO. RIF.

(Continued)
Part 2

From 10 p.m. 25.9.15 - 3 a.m.
Part 2.

25/26

1. During the night the troops continued to improve the trenches with all available implements and tools. About 10 p.m. the Germans made a fairly determined counter-attack but it was easily repulsed.

There were heavy bursts of rifle and Machine Gun fire on the right of the line probably owing to the German counter-attacks.

2. About 4.30 a.m. the first lines of the 21st Division appeared through the mist.

3. The bombardment of the German Trenches commenced about 8 a.m. and lasted well over the half-hour, a fair proportion of shells fell among our troops.
This demoralized the troops supporting our left who retired but they were soon rallied.

4. At the end of the bombardment, the order was given for the assault but on the left it had no effect.

5. There followed a retirement of the troops acting on our left which left Puits No 14 bis. and buildings at H. 31 b.2.7 unprotected. Consequently the enemy established themselves there with Machine Guns.

From 10 p.m. 25.9.15 - 3 a.m.

6. Between 11 a.m. and 3 p.m. on 26 Sep, the chief events were advances retirements of the 21st Division; each advance was accompanied by rapid fire from the rear on our Trenches.
Meanwhile the Germans were reinforced in there positions on our left and so enfiladed us.

7. Our artillery kept up a consistent fire on these positions and those on our immediate front.

8. About 5 p.m. a retirement commenced on our right which was followed by an order to retire to the 45th Brigade who were then practically the only troops on the Hill.

9. This retirement was stopped by the arrival of the Royal Dragoons in LOOS and the position on Hill 70 was immediately reoccupied.

10. About 3 a.m. there was a general order to the 15th Division to withdraw to QUALITY STREET.

In the Field
  28.9.15   (Sgd)

          J.C. Grant, Captain
          A La T. Baillie, Captain
          W.L. Renwick Captain
           10th Sco. Rif.

7° K O S B's
N° 4 Column
28.9.15

B

NARRATIVE

Re your B.M. 926 aaa The 7th K.O.S.B.
advanced on the 25th at 6.30 a.m.
Two platoons one from each of the leading
companies formed the 1st line, then 2 more,
and so on . Thus three lines in all advanced .
The lines at the start were about 50 yds apart
but on reaching the 1st German lines the rear
lines had gained so much on the 1st lines that
the number of lines at that time was really two.
The interval in the 1st Line was then about 1 yd.
between men owing to casualties.

Bombers were with the leading two coys and
bombed support and Communicating trenches
catching many German in dug outs. A reliable
Sergt. states he counted 14 dead in one dug
out . Casualties were very slight during
bombardment, but immediately the advance started
casualties were very heavy (especially among
officers) from Shrapnel and Machine Gun fire .

After crossing the German 2nd line very few
casualties occurred until after crossing the
crest of Hill 70, and the retirement back over
it again where they became very heavy. aaa
The small redoubt on Hill 70 though heavily
wired, and untouched by our artillery appears
to have been hardly held by the Germans at all,
and caused very little bother AAA.

The cause of the losses after advancing over
Hill 70 was undoubtedly caused by largely by
flanking fire as it appears that a message was

passed along that a battalion on 7th Bn K.O.S.B. right had taken a village — The 7th Bn K.O.S.B. thought this meant CITE ST AUGUSTE whereas it was LOOS. The men cheered loudly and charged forward mistaking Germans who were removing guns from near CITE AUGUSTE for the Black Watch.

The battalion was not held up until after it passed over Hill 70, our artillery giving great support.

After crossing Hill 70 artillery fire on both sides seemed to cease.

Germans appeared to be very frightened immediately the men got to close quarters with them, and many were bayoneted.

The transport suffered their casualties on the afternoon 25th September when ordered up with ammunition to LOOS by coming across one of our trenches across the road, thus causing a halt at a time when the German Artillery were playing on them.

My information is from Lt. NEWBIGGING, and our M.O. and Transport Officers.

                     (Sgd) C. Connell, Major
                     Commanding 7th K.O.S.B.

5 p.m.

No 5 Column.
12th H.L.I.

Report on Operations of A. and B. Companies and
M.G. Section 12th Bn High. L.I. during attack
25th and 26th September.

At the commencement of operations on 25th September
A. and B. Companies 12th Bn High. L.I. forming the 5th
Column and commanded by Captain P.W. Torrance were in
position in our front line trench, A. Coy. on the right
B. Coy. on the left, the frontage covered extending from
the VERMELLE-LOOS ROAD on the right to the LE RUTOIRE
LOOS ROAD on the left.
They were supported by four Machine Guns, two of which were
kept under cover until such time as they should advance.

The objective of No 5 Column was the German front
line, communication and support trenches from LOOS ROAD
REDOUBT to SOUTHERN SAP, which when taken by the Infantry
were to be consolidated and held, the Machine Guns being
brought up for this purpose. At 6.30 a.m. on the morning
of the 25th September immediately on cessation of the Gas
A. and B. companies sent sections of Infantry forward
supported by Machine Gun fire, to make way for the bombers
who were to clear the German trenches in LOOS ROAD REDOUBT
and the SOUTHERN SAP respectively. Owing to the condition
of the wind and the contour of our line on the right,
many of A. company's men suffered from the effects of
our own gas before leaving the trenches.
B. Company were also apparently affected by it, but not
to the same extent. SOUTHERN SAP on investigation
proved to be only a track some few inches deep and was
responsible for many of the losses sustained by B.

company, who had looked for shelter in it. It was
raked by Machine Gun fire constantly. All the company's
Officers were killed, and all its sergeants either killed
or wounded before reaching the German lines wire , but the
Bombers got through and proceeded with their work of
clearing the trenches and eventually met in with those of
A. Company . On account of the losses sustained and a
shortage of bombs, it was impossible to carry out the
original idea of bombing along the trenches to the left
to get into touch with the Bombers of the 1st Division who
failed to put in an appearance.

Acting on orders from O.C. Column the Machine Guns were
brought forward at 7.15 a.m. but owing to the German front
line trenches being still held in places by the enemy ,
they met with considerable opposition both from Machine
Gun and rifle fire. Three of our guns gained the trenches
with about 30% of casualties but the fourth on the right
and in charge of the M.G.O. was put out of action, being
struck by a bullet, and the section at this point reduced
to two men. Pte A. Ramage (17641) Acting No 1 on No 4 Gun
is deserving of special mention for the cool and able
manner he displayed in handling the gun under fire. At
about 11.30 a.m. M.G.O. and SIGS entered the German front
line trench at a point just N. of SOUTHERN SAP and found
O.C. Column and some 80 men of A and B Eompanies barricading
the fire trench, as a party of the enemy were still holding
about 50 yds of their trench to our N. Two machine guns of
ours were covering operations at the time. About noon a
bombing party of 6th Camerons arrived and endeavoured to
clear the trench, with partial success. During this
period the support line and firexstepsxxxds was put in a
state of defence and emplacements and fire steps made and
Machine Guns mounted.

About 3.30 p.m. some of the 1st Division arrived and completed the clearing of this trench. At 5 p.m. the 1st Division passed through. Owing to the 1st Division Bombers not appearing the 5th Column found its position too much to the left and proceeded to occupy the frontage allotted to in Brigade Orders, which was put in a state of defence and held during the night 25/26th Sept. About 9.30 a.m. on the 26th September O.C. Column received orders tp change his position and eventually took up a line in an enemy trench 36 B G.29.c.39 to G.29.B.03. This position was held until the evening of 26th September when orders were received for the troops to be withdrawn.

(Sgd) J.H.Purvis, Lt. Col.

1.10.15.   Commanding, 12th Bn High. L.I.

Head Quarters
46th Inf. Bde.

I submit a report received from Capt Tourance - who commanded N° 5 Column on 25th Sept. — The previous report enclosed was drawn up by Lt Laird in Capt Tourance's absence.

J. N. Purvis Lt. Col.
Comd 12th Highl. L.I.

13·10·15

Report of the O.C. No.5 Column
25th and 26th September 1915.

The gas attack commenced at 5.5 a.m. on the 25th.

Unfortunately two (or three) of the gas cylinders burst and several more were leaky and we had several casualties through men being gassed.

This I can only attribute to carelessness as the helmets were most efficient.

At 6.30 a.m. prompt the assault began. I could see the left, or "B" assaulting party deploying but owing to the thickness of the smoke I was unable to see the right, or "A" party, going out. Owing to the smoke, visual signalling was impossible, and as I had no word from either "A" or "B" party, at about 6.50 a.m. I sent across a runner to each party for information. Neither of these runners returned. At about 7.10 a.m., after speaking to the Brigade Major on the telephone, I was about to take my reserve over to the German trenches when I received word from both "A" and "B" Company Commanders. From "A" Company that the German front line and support trenches were taken, and from "B" Coy that Southern Sap was taken. I immediately sent on these messages to the Brigade and at once proceeded across with the Reserve, half of which I sent by Southern Sap, and the other half I took myself by LOOS ROAD REDOUBT.

On arriving in the German trenches I found they were indeed taken, but the casualties were very heavy. I found myself the only unwounded Officer there. I set the men with me at work fire stepping and reversing the parapet in the German support trench and made my way to the north of Southern Sap, where our men under the

direction/

direction of C.S.M.Bruce "A" Company were bombing up the German front line and support trenches. We had cleared about 100 yards of these trenches to the north of SOUTHERN SAP when we ran out of bombs, so many of the bomb carriers having become casualties on the way across to the German trenches. We were able to secure a quantity of German bombs, but as the quantity of these was limited, and the force at my disposal had suffered so severely and was inadequate to hold the section of trenches allotted to us I decided to stop the offensive till I got more bombs and bombers. I sent messages to the Brigade asking for these to be sent. The position at this time was rather critical. The Germans counter attacked strongly down their front line trench, but we had blocked this trench, and L/Cpl Anderson of "A" Coy made some excellent practice with the German bombs. The enemy made an attempt to come at us across the open between the front line and support trenches, but we had got our machine guns mounted in a communication trench, and we had no difficulty in keeping the Germans from coming out.

Shortly after this the M.G.O. Lt. Laird and the Signal Officer Lt. Hawley got across to the trenches we were occupying and they were both of great assistance to me. Bombs were now coming across to us, brought by a party under Sgt.McGarry and we were able to resume the offensive. About 11 o'clock, a bombing party of the 6th Camerons under 2nd.Lt.Watson came to our assistance and this Officer led the bomb attack up the German front line, and C.S.M.Bruce of "A" Coy led the bomb attack up the German support line. In this way we cleared another 300 yards of the German trenches in the 1st Divisional Area, but as there was still no

Sign/

sign of the 1st Divisional Bombers meeting us, I ordered the trenches to be blocked again, as I considered that in the event of a heavy counter attack across the open, we would be holding too wide a front for the number of men we had. About three o'clock in the afternoon the 1st. Divisional Troops came across, and I withdrew my Command and occupied the trenches allotted to No.5 Column in 46th Brigade Operation Order No.11. My dispositions were:-
H.L.I. in the front line or original German Support trench, Camerons in the original German firing line trench. The usual night sentries were posted, and most of the night was spent in making fire steps.

On the morning of the 26th, on the authority of the Brigade Major, I sent back parties to LENS ROAD KEEP to get water. Dixies came up from QUALITY STREET with tea and provisions which the men shared with the Camerons. After breakfast, in accordance with orders received from the Brigade, I was proceeding with my command to the place allotted to us when I saw a retiral over on the right near the LENS ROAD and, knowing that there were some of our own troops in front of us, I moved up to the German second line trench in front of LOOS, and reported to the Brigadier in this trench about 200 yards north of the VERMELLES - LOOS Road. There I received orders from the Brigadier to take up a defensive position across the VERMELLES - LOOS Road, and to report to him when this was done. This would be about 10 a.m.. I was on my way back to report to the Brigadier that this had been done when I was knocked down by the explosion of an H.E. shell close to me.

When I got to my senses and reached the place where I had left the Brigadier he was gone, but I reported to the Brigade M.G.O.

7. 10. 15.   Sgd. P.W.TORRANCE.

12th H L I

Short Narrative of events 25th/26th Sept. 1915.

On the morning of the 25th the 12th Bn High. L.I. was in position in the trenches as ordered, A and B companies occupying a position in front line system, forming the 5th attacking column, C and D Coys being in support to 10th Bn Sco. Rifles (3rd Col) and 7th Bn K.O.Sco. Bord. (4th Col.) respectively. C. and D. Coys occupied C.T. 16.

I have no personal knowledge of the actions of the 5th attacking column and propose to deal only with the situation as I found it in my immediate vicinity.

C. Coy. moved up to the front system followed by D, and reached the front line parapet without a hitch.

The last of the leading Battalions had just left.

I then ordered my two Coys to advance in support and they cross over to the German trenches.

From this point we advanced towards our objective without a pause until we reinforced the firing line in the neighbourhood of Puit 14 (Bis) This was taken by our left flank without opposition.

At this time I was on the extreme left and realised our line was gradually changing to a more Southerly direction and advancing on LENS instead of CITE ST AUGUSTE . Our left advancing along the LE BASSEE -LENS ROAD in place of the road running

2.

East, marked " Metalled, but poor "
Further we were not in touch with the first
Division which should have been on our immediate
left at PUIT 14 (Bis) and our left flank was
dangerously exposed.
These facts were reported by me to the Brigade
at the time.

At this moment I saw Major Glenny of the
7th Bn K.O.Sco. Bord. and told him that we must
endeavour to bring the attack back to the right
direction and delay advancing until this was
accomplished. He agreed with me and said he
would get this carried out. The line was now
continuing direct on Hill 70. . Just before
reaching the road junction at 31.B.3.5. I saw my
orders were not being carried out and that the line
had advanced too near the crest of the Hill. I then
sent Captain Stevenson to Major Glenny to tell him
I did not consider he should advance further, but
should halt and get the line consolidated. Major
Glenny told Captain Stevenson that he had no
intention of going further.

I then sat down at the road junction (31. B
3.5.) and wrote a lengthy report of the situation.
On getting up from this I found the whole of the
firing line had passed over the crest of Hill 70.
I immediately proceeded over the crest of the
hil and found that they were hotly engaged with
the enemy holding the line in front of the CITE ST
LAURENT and were being driven back by Machine Gun
fire. I sat down to write a report to the Brigade
and before I had finished it most of the line
had retired . They were then rallied

behind a small enbankment running East and West just below the crest of the hill, where they dug themselves in. At this period realising the weakness of our exposed left flank I took steps to protect this by placing troops in the wood South of BOIS HUGO and PUIT 14 (Bis), and also occupied BOIS HUGO itself.

This was the state of affairs at nightfall on the 25th.

That night about 9 p.m. I proceeded to Brigade Headquarters to report situation. I then learned the 62nd Brigade was to co-operate with us in the defence of Hill 70. but that touch could not be obtained with this Brigade.

On my way back from Headquarters I met some of the 62nd Brigade and eventually fell in with the 13th Northumberland Fusiliers whose Adjutant said they were looking for the Brigadier, 46th Brigade, and that they were to come under his orders.

I then guided them to a point when on the road 30.N.2.1. and explained the whole situation to their C.O.

With the exception of one Company they remained here for the night. The Company was sent up to strengthen our left front. They dug themselves in on the North side of the wood at (B.31.5.8.)

At this stage I sent a message to Brigade Headquarters, reporting situation but received no acknowledgement.

At 2 a.m. I went myself to report to the Brigadier.

The situation, therefore, of all troops at Hill 70 on the morning of the 26th was precisely the same as at nightfall on the 25th excepting that we had been reinforced by one Battalion (13th Northumberland Fusiliers)

When the Hill was shelled by our guns on the morning of 26th the troops holding the trench just under the crest were badly shelled by our own guns and in some places shelled out of it, and were also fired on by some of the relieving troops.

From this time onward I can make no statement as to any definite movement being carried out.

The proceedings resolved themselves into stray bodies of men being rallied and collected by any Officer in their vicinity.

Eventually we were driven back to the South side of the LOOS-HULLOCH " road.

I then went in search of my No 5 Column which had been left in the German Trenches Not finding it I went on to Quality Street. where I collected 120 men, these I took up to our front line trenches where we remained until relieved at 10 p.m. the same evening.

29.9.15.
(Sgd) J.H. Purvis. Lt.Cd
Commanding 12th Bn High. L.I.

8th KOSB

(1) The 8th Bn K.C.S.B's were in reserve to the 46th Bde on the attack on the German lines on 25th September. Two platoons of each C. and D. Coys were detailed for digging and making the two Russian saps into C.T. to the German lines. The distance appears to have been wrongly estimated, as the distance to be dug was more than 400 yds in both cases. Consequently this work was not completed although the men worked from 7 a.m. until 8.30 pm. Part of the time men were taken for carrying ammunition up to firing line. These four platoons returned to Quality Street night of 25/26th and were there detained by order of Staff Officer of 44th Bde on Sunday 26th. The digging platoons emerged from the the trenches, one party after the H.L.I. had got out of our fire trench, the other before the H.L.I. got out.

(2) The remaining two platoons of each C. and D Coys. were told to cross over the trenches after the H.L.I., followed by A. and B. Coys. C. Coy. was on the right C.T. No 12 and 25, D. Coy was on the left C.T. Northern Up 15 and 14. D. Coy $\frac{1}{2}$ Coy was detained by me at the point of 15 C trench nearest to LOOS ROAD Keep where instructions from Brigade were awaited. Orders from me to advance were sent to C. and A. Coy. These orders I have reason to believe were not received by C. or A. Coy. as they crossed the front line trench about $\frac{1}{4}$ to $\frac{1}{2}$ an hour before left column.

The order from G.O.C. 46th Bde was that as the leading line had taken and occupied German first line trench, the reserve Battalion would follow over after the H.L.I.

On arriving at our first line trench thich I did by crossing over the top of the trenches I could find no sign of the H.L.I. nor of my right column. I told the O.C. D and B Coys to hurry up and follow up the H.L.I. and I went in search of my right column.

As this could not be found I supposed it had gone on ahead.

The half of D Coy. appears to have marched on left of 46th Bde line and to have reached H. 31.b.3.5. A platoon was sent part of the way along road rigx H. 31.b.3.5. to H. 32. a.7.9. . As the right of the line advanced D. Coy conformed to the movement crossing over the top of the hill along HULLOCH-LENS road . Not long afterwards these men and in fact the whole of the left of the line were seen to be withdrawing . This half Coy. now became mixed up with other units; its Captain was wounded at the time.

B Coy was to have followed D Coy in two lines of ½ Coys but as it was found that the left of the firing line had not joined up with the 1st Division, Captain Cruickshank was ordered to dig trenches and to place two houses in a state of defence. This was only partially done and part of the Coy. appears to have joined up with the line which was attacking Hill 70 and the remainder to have moved a little xxx more South, after some of the 9th Bn Gordon Highlanders had prolonged a little the line to the left of 46th Inf. Bde front, towards Chalk Pit wood. At 4 p.m. Captain Cruickshank ordered one platoon to skirmish a short way through BOIS HUGO, at the same time he was seen to go off by himself with a rifle and bayonet. He has not been seen since. From the evening of 25th till early morning 40 men of B Coy. were under charge of Lt. Herbertson and had taken up a position on the South side of PUITS 14 bis- men of the battalion were collected and joined up with this party till it numbered about 80 men together with 2nd Lt. Pelham. They remained in this position until the 6th Camerons retired when they retired with them.

The remaining half of C. Coy. emerged from the trenches which had been occupied by the 10th Bn Sco. Rif. This column appears to have followed the course of the leading troops. The commander was early wounded and ½ Coy. left to the command of a 2nd Lieut. who took it on and over Hill 70 where he was wounded and is now missing. The men who remained joined with men of other Corps and a few men remained on Hill 70 till Sunday night when they withdrew to LOOS and later to Quality Street.

A Coy. which should have followed C. Coy down the communicating trenches appears to have taken the wrong C.T. trench and later to have got on top of our own trench line and to have followed with the rest of the 46th Bde line of attack. It was carried too far to the west. This Coy. went through the outskirts of LOOS and bombed several houses. The Company Commander was wounded quite early in the day. The Company was then led by its 2nd in Command up to a point South of Hill 70 about N 1 a.6.6 where he was killed as also his subaltern. The men of this Coy. along with men of other Units appear to have retired to the northern edge of Hill 70. The leading men of A. Coy. went along C.T. 12 and became separated from the rest of the Coy. These men marched on Chalk Pit Wood and turned half right joining the firing line on Hill 70.

In consequence of the separation of the Battn moving along the C. Trenches in two columns -control was lost. The Battalion emreged from the trenches in different places. A large working party reduced the size of the Battalion. These columns instead of acting as a reserve became early merged into the firing line and went on with it over Hill 70

The machine guns of the Battalion moved across the front in the rear of the H.L.I. and early joined the firing line. No 2 Section gun was out of action at the time of the first retirement back to Hill 70, was speedily repaired broken part removed and carried back on to Hill 70. Nothing more has been heard of this section or the gun.

No 3 Section did good work from corner house at Puits 14 bis it was withdrawn when this portion of the line retired. The Sergeant with his two men remaining attached himself to the 6th Cameron Highlanders. The gun appears to have been lost in the retirement. No 4 Gun under Lt. Surtees was taken over Hill 70. On retirement the Gun No 2, who was carrying the gun was wounded, the gun remaining with him.

28.9.15

(Sgd) T.B.Sellar, Lt.Col
Commdg 8th Bn K.O.S.B.

Report by Major H. POLLARD-LOWSLEY C.I.E., R.E.
on the operation of the 24th to 27th inst.

Reference 1/10,000 Trench Map 36 c N.W. - sheets 3 and part of 1.

1. This report deals, so far as I am in a position to do so, with the work of H. Company of the 9th Gordons (Pioneers) in conjunction with the 91st Field Coy. R.E. Owing to the fact that, except in the case of Nos 14 and 16 Platoons, touch was lost between Platoons and Sections immediately after our troops passed our front line, and to the fact that all officers of the ~~ENE~~ H Company have become casualties, it is impossible now to collect anything like a complete account of the doings of this Company.

2. Distribution of Company. In accordance with 46th Infantry Brigade Order No 11 dated 15.9.15 H. Company 9th Gordon Highlanders (Pioneers) with the 91st Field Coy. R.E. was distributed as follows :--

No 1 Section. 91st Field Coy. R.E. (Lieut. DAVENPORT R.E.) with No 16 Platoon 9th Gordons (2nd Lt. MACGREGOR) reserve to No 3 Column.

No 2 Section 91st Field Coy. R.E. (Lieut. McCOURT RME.) with No 14 Platoon 9th Gordons 2nd Lt. BISSETT) reserve to No 4 Column.

No 3 Section 91st Field Coy. R.E. (Lieut. McNaught R.E.) with No 13 Platoon 9th Gordons (2nd Lieut Murray) with No 3 Column.

No 4 Section 91st Field Coy. R.E. (Lieut. J.A. Parker R.E.) with No 15 Platoon 9th Gordons (2nd Lieut Pitcairn) with No 4 Column. Captain A.P. Sayer R.E. (91st Field Coy. R.E.) and Captain MaxWhirter O.C. H. Coy. 9th Gordons were posted with Nos 1 and 2 sections and the attached platoons with the Reserve.

2. Movements. Under the original orders of the G.O.C. 46th Inf. Bde. Nos 1 and 2 Sections other attached platoons (16 and 14) were due to enter NORTHERN UP trench at MAZINGARBE at 7.30 p.m. on the 24th September and Nos 3 and 4 Sections with Nos 13 and 15 Platoons at 9.15 p.m. At 6 p.m. on the 24th orders were received to stand fast. At 8.30 p.m. orders were received to carry out on and new times for starting were fixed. Nos 1 and 2 sections of the 91st Field Coy. R.E. with Nos 14 and 16 Platoons 9th Gordons left MAZINGARBE at 9.30 p.m. with Captain MacWhirter and under Captain Sayer R.E. They marched overland to PHILOSOPHE where they entered NORTHERN UP and proceeded to their allotted positions in C.T. 16 . Nos 3 and 4 Sections of the 91st Field Coy. R.E. with No 13 and 15 Platoons, 9th Gordons followed at 10.45 p.m. and took up their positions in C.T's 15 and 16 respectively.

3. At 4.5 a.m. on the 25th September the O.C. 91st Field Coy. R.E. received information from the 46th Inf. Bde. that the gas discharge would commence at 5.50 a.m. and the assault would take place at 6.30 a.m. These orders were communicated to all Section Officers who were instructed to inform their attached Platoon Officers of the 9th Gordons. Consequent on the change in time for the assault it became necessary to alter starting time for sections and platoons. Times were altered to the following and communicated to Captain Sayer for Nos 1 and 2 Sections and their attached Platoons and to the section officers of Nos 3 and 4 sections direct for communication to their Platoon Officers.

No 3 Sec. and No 13 Platoon   5.47 a.m.

No 4 Sec. and No 15 Platoon   5.53 a.m.

Nos 1 and 2 Sections and Nos 14
         and 16 Platoons   6.45 a.m.

Times of strating of the 8th Bn K.O.Sco. Bord. cols 3 and 4 were also communicated.

4. All sections and Platoons moved off at the times fixed and all took up their allotted positions in the columns. Two parties each consisting of 2 sappers and 6 Pioneers from Sections 1 and 2 of the 91st Field Coy. R.E. and Platoons 16 and 14 of the 9th Gordons proceeded to the Russian Sap in Fire Bays 24 and 131 near C.T's 9.B. and 9 and started work with the two leading Platoons of the 8th Bn K.O.Sco. Bord. in each column on opening up three saps and continuing them as Communication Trenches to connect our front trenches with the German front Trenches. At about 9 a.m. work on these Trenches was inspected by Captain A.F. Sayer R.E. who found that sufficient men had not been employed on them. He collected more men, obtained tools for them from near R.E. Trench Store No 2 and put them on the work. These trenches were completed furing the day though work was for some time interferred with by rifle and shrapnel fire.

5. No 13 Platoon . No record of anyb kind can be obtained regarding the doings of this platoon . Presumably it left the front line trenches at about 7 a.m. with No 3 Section and probably it met immediately with heavy casualties In the case of No 3 Section , the Section Officer (Lt MacNaught) and all N.C.O's with the exception of one Lance Corporal was hit before the German Front line was reached and in the absence of evidence , a similar fate must be presumed to have been met by No 13 Platoon.

6. No 15 Platoon.   In the case of this Platoon also I can obtain no record of its fate . Lieut. Parker did not see the Platoon out of our trenches nor did he see it afterwards. Lieut Parker , however, himself took a wrong course and proceeded too far to the north entering the area allotted to No 5 Column .

He   suffer/ed very heavy casualties (16) which virtually knocked his section out for the day; but it may be that No 15 Platoon took a more correct course and got through without serious casualtied . None of my officers, however, came across the Platoon during the day.

7. No 16 Platoon (2nd Lt MacGregor, 9th Gordons)
This platoon left our front line trenches at about 7.45 a.m. immediately in rear of No 1 sec. of the 91st Field Coy. R.E. (Lieut. Davenport R.E.).
The point at which they left is near the junction of the front line with C.T. 9.   The platoon then advanced in line with and on the left of Sec. No 1. Lieuts Davenport and 2nd Lt. MacGregor being within speaking distance of one another. The proceeded to H. 31 a.27 where they halted to allow the 8th Bn K.O.Sco. Bord. to pass . It appears that the 8th Bn K.O.Sco. Bord. had taken a wrong turn in our trenches and that this had resulted in No 16 Platoon and No 1 Section getting out of place. Here Capt. MacWhirter formed the party, having himself advanced up to this point with No 2 Section and No 14 Platoon. Captain MacWhirter took No 16 Platoon off to the left but Lieut. Davenport realisibg that if he followed he would leave his correct line of advance stopped where he was. Shortly afterwards Capt. MacWhirter returned to Lieut. Davenport and instructed him to put in a state of defence a house at the chalk pit (H. 25.a.95) . He hi

5.

H. 25.a.9.5.). He himself (Captain MacWhirter) had been ordered by Col. Sellar or possibly Col. Purvis, it is not clear which to dig in on the left flank on a line extending from H. 25.A.95 to PUITS 14 bis and to hold it When Lieut. Davenport proceeded to place this house in a state of defence he again joined up therefore with No 16 Platoon. The Pioneers completed digging in and between 5 and 6 p.m. the line was taken over by the 2nd Brigade in whose area it was situated.

At about 6.30 p.m. Captain MacWhirter received orders from the O.C. 6th Bn Cameron Highlanders to fill the gap between PUITS No 14 bis and the houses at H. 31.b.29 along the West side of the LENS BENIFONTAINE road. No 16 Platoon and No 1 Section 91st Field Coy. R.E. both took up this work. At 9 p.m. orders were received to move across this road and dig in on the East side of it. This also was done, No 16 Platoon filling up the gap in the line and No 1 Section digging on behind them.

This line was held until about 11 a.m. on the 26th inst. when an order came from the left to retire. No 16 Platoon and No 1 Section retired together after all other troops had left.

The section and Platoon became separated on the retirement and neither Lt. Davenport nor any of his men have seen wither Captain MacWhirter or Lieut. MacGregor or any of No 16 Platoon since then. Both the platoon and the section were split up on the retirement.

8. No 14 Platoon. (2nd Lt. BISSETT). This platoon left the front line trenches with No 2 Section of the 91st Field Coy. R.E.(Lieut. McCourt R.E.) at about 8.15 a.m.

at about 8.15 a.m. on the 25th inst. The point at which they left was between C.T. 12 and Boyau 9.B. They followed the Russian Sap from Bay 24 to the German front line trenches, No 2 Section leaving and No 14 Platoon following. At this point Lieut. McCourt called a halt and waited for No 14 platoon which arrived soon afterwards with Captain MacWhirter who then gave the order to advance as far as possible. The platoon and section proceeded together along a line G. 28.b.03 G.30.a.00 G.30.d.06 G.30.d.80. H.31.a.30 to H. 31.c.61.

The point H. 31 c.61 near the crest of Hill 70 was reached at about 9 a.m. Here Lieut. McCourt called a halt and made his men lie down as they were under a heavy rifle fire. Lieut Bissett and his platoon conformed to this, but after a few minutes he advanced over the crest with his men. Neither he nor his men appear to have returned. They must have come under an extremely hot fire immediately they got over the crest and Lt. McCourt reports that he has seen nothing of them since then.

9. Recommendation. In the absence of complete information regarding the doing of H Company of the 9th Gordons it is difficult to make specific recommendations. The only platoon of whose doings there is any connected record is Platoon No 16. The platoon working with No 1 Section of the 91st Field Coy. has undoubtedly done some excellent and useful work and Captain MacWhirter and 2nd Lt. MacGregor are entitled to all credit for this work. I am unable to say whether anyb of the N.C.O's or men of H Company specially distinguished themselves as I have been unable to get into touch with any of them. I understand that the company has been almost entirely wiped out and that very few men now remain.

10. Work Done. With the exception of Platoon 16 which has done good Pioneer work it does not appear that any Platoon has done any such work. It is possible that Platoons 13 and 15 even, as in the case of my sections 3 and 4 which they accompanied, so badly knocked about as to be incapicitated for further work. No 14 Platoon would perhaps have been available for Pioneer work when required later had 2nd Lt. Bissett not allowed them to proceed beyond the crest of Hill 70. H. Company has displayed a high standard of discipline and a most commendable desire to come to close quarters with the enemy. This desire must , however, be curbed if the men are to be available for use as Pioneers when wanted by the Infantry .

I have no figures for casualties suffered.

(Sgd) J.Pollard-Lowsley
Major,
91st Field Coy. R.E.

29-9-15.

Report by Captain A.P. Sayer R.E.
91st Field Company R.E.
on Operations from 24.9.15 to 27.9.15

Reference to Trench Map 36.c. N.W. 3 and Part of 1
1/10,000

24.9.15.

7.30 p.m.   Ordered "Stand by " for Company in accordance with message from 46th Inf. Bde. Informed H. Coy. 9th Gordons Highlanders (Pioneers) attached to this company.

8.30 p.m.   Orders for move received from 46th Inf. Bde. Issued orders to Company and Pioneers.

9.30 p.m.   Parade with Nos 1 and 2 Sections. Captain MacWhistler reports with Nos 14 and 16 platoons H. Company 9th Gordon Hghrs.

9.45 p.m.   Marched out overland to PHILOSOPHE and by Northern Up Trench and 16.

11.15 p.m. Arrived at allotted position in No 16 C.T.

25-9-15.

1.0 a.m.   Received programme of assault.

4.0 a.m.   Received Time Table for attack ; issued orders to Sections and Pioneers.

6.0 a.m.	Moved up C.T. 16 in rear of High. L.I. to Northern Up.
6.45 a.m.	Moved up C.T. 15 . Later I found that 1½ companies 6th Cameron Hghrs (part of Divisional Reserve) had got in ahead of my party and was blocking my
8.30 a.m.	progress . Eventually succeeded in extricating my party and proceeded in proper position. On arrival at Front Line Trench I quitted this party and took Sergt. Hay and two orderlies to inspect work on converting Russian Saps.
9.0 a.m.	Found work proceeding well on Russian Sap insufficient number of men at work to connect up with German Front Line. I obtained parties from the Companies of 6th Bn Cameron Highlanders , who were occupying Fire and Support Trenches, and tools from R.E. Trench Store No 2 and put men to work. Working parties at this time were being considerably interfered with by snipers and later by Shrapnell Message from Lt. Parker, No 4 Section reporting that he was held up in front of German Trenches about G.22.D.22 North of LCOS ROAD REDOUBT , as he was out of direction I ordered him to withdraw if possible and move up to Hill 70 and join his column.
10.15 a.m.	Returned to our trenches and found 14 men No 3 Section who reported having lost

all N.C.O's and their Section Officer Lt.
MacNaught with the exception of Lc Cpl. Melvin
Put Sergt Hay in command and reported to O.C.
at Advanced Brigade Headquarters at junction of
trenches 22 and 26.

10.30 a.m. Took up this party (No 3 Section)
via LOOS ROAD through German trenches ; turned
off to about G. 29.b.2.3. where I found
Brigadier 46th Inf. Bde. and forward Headquarters.
Reported and received instructions to send up all
available Sappers to forward troops on Hill 70
to assist in entrenching the position .
At German 1st Reserve line I found a Company
6th Camerons occupying trench and instructed them
to prepare it for defence and to move the
German chevaur de frise into position. This was
about line G. 28.b.7.1. to G. 28 B.9.5.

11.15 a.m. Moved forward and collected party
of No 2 Section . Corpl Bannister and 5 men who
had been sent off from their Section. Took this
party forward with No 3 Section.
On reaching about point G. 30 c.1.8. troops on
Hill 70 Northern Slope up to about PUITS 14 bis
appeared to be falling back so I commenced to
convert a group of Machine Gun emplacements and
Field Gun emplacements into fire position for a
supporting point.
After a short time the troops appeared to have
removed their position on ridge so in accordance
with the Generals instructions I sent Corporal
Bannister and his party up to left part of line
with directions to reconnoitre wood running

N.E. from G.30.d.99 with a view to entrenching
a line northwards from Puits 14 bis tomprotect
left flank of our line, and to report to O.C.
of troops on left.

I also directed Sergt. Hay to take No 3 Section
up to group of houses at G. 36.b.87 and prepare
them for defence, and if troops still held their
position to go up to Hill 70 and place the section
at disposal of Infantry Officer holding line below
work at 31 central.

1.15 p.m.   :Returned to our lines and reported O.C
at Brigade Headquarters Advance Station.

2.30 p.m.   Proceeded to Brigade Headquarters at
forward Station (G. 29.b.2.3.) and reported to
Brigadier. Remained at his disposal and assisted
in Brigade Staff work. Kept Headquarters open
during absence of Brigadier.

9.30 p.m.   Returned with Brigadier to LOOS ROAD KEEP

NOTES. (25.9.15.)

1. After advance of assaulting columns no great
effort appeared to be made to search and clear
German trenches. A considerable amount of sniping
from these trenches occurred throughout the
morning. At about 11 a.m. two German Officers and
10 men came out of a dug out in Front line of
LOOS ROAD REDOUBT and surrendered to me. I sent
them in with an escort.

2. Bridges over our Front trenches for the

5.

passage of wounded and also direction boards to Dressing stations were required more frequently. The Fire trench became blocked in places by wounded.

3. I received no reports from Corpl Bannister as to his work after I had sent him off at about 12.45 p.m. nor from Sergt Hay until 7 p.m., when I sent him and party to bring up sandbags for use of the troops entrenching line below Hill 70 work, these were never sent up chiefly owing to fatigue of men and lack of carriers.

4. Sergt. Hay's work in Houses at G.36.b.87 was not very complete only loopholes and fire steps being provided and a small amount of internal communication.

5. German trenches did not appear any good except the main communication trenches to rear which were 6 feet deep generally and had good arrangements for drainage by means of frequent sump pits with wooden gratings. Their telephone wire in these trenches did not appear to be buried or let into sides of trench.
The artillery work on wire cutting was very effective.

26/9/15.
7.0. a.m.   Proceeded with Brigadier and O.C. to Advanced Headquarters at G.29.b.23. On arrival parties of 46th Infantry Brigade were found returning from Hill 70 having been relieved. Brigadier ordered

them to be collected and taken back to positions to support troops who were to attack ridge and work of Hill 70. Acting under his instructions I collected one N.C.O. and about 30 men of Units of the 46th Inf. Bde. and took them up to the GRENAY-BENIFONTAINE ROAD about G.29.b.9.a. Here I collected other stragglers from 44th and 45th Brigades and also from SOMERSETS and DURHAMS. Under instructions from Brigadier 46th Inf. Bde I took this party now mustering about 3 N.C.O's and 120 men at about 8.45 a.m. upto road LOOS-HULLUCH lining the bank immediately South of a battery of howitzers.

At about 9.15 a.m. a company of, I believe ROYAL SCOTS, who had lines the road on my right, moved forward up the hill in two lines. I presumed that they were advancing to carry forward the attack on the ridge that should have taken place at 9.0 a.m. and as their left appeared to be edging off to the right I decided to take up my party to cover their left flank. This appeared to me to be necessary as some heavy firing commenced from a point North of the work on Hill 70 and some Germans appeared advancing on skyline about H.31.b.26.

When about half way up to road marked " Metalled but poor " a number of Germans retired over summit of hill from work at 31 central and the party to the North of Work also appeared to have fallen back. Our advance was subjected to heavy rifle fire and to Machine Gun fire from about H.31.b.27 and also to Shrapnel from the North, probably HULLUCH or its vicinity.

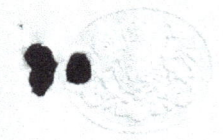

On arrival at our trenches I found them crowded with a varied collection of troops and a large proportion were SOMERSETS . I called on these troops to advance and charge. The distance was only about 50 yds and the wire was not strong. Only the Scottish troops followed and being met with a very severe fire I was obliged to fall back to our trenches. A subsequent effort failed in the same way being only supported by the few Scottish troops on the left. Shortly after this a German movement commenced on North of our position but this was stopped by Machine Gun fire and by returning my left flank slightly N.W. and the advance of several lines of troops up the hill between my position and PUITS 14 bis appeared to make this safe.

Moving along towards the right I endeavoured to get the two officers of the SOMERSETS to take their men forward , the men complained of being done up and wanting food.

I met Captain Grant , 10th Bn Sco. Rif. moving from right, he had with him a subaltern of the same battalion We decided to take charge of the situation as none of the other officers whom we had seen appeared sufficiently capable . Shortly afterwards a German attack took place south of the work on H. 31 central and our troops on right gave way. We rallied them and Captain Grant took them back to their line again.

I got into communication with Brigade Major, 46th I.B. on telephone and reported position . Orders to hang on. At about 10.30 a.m. the troops on our left suddenly began to give way and to retreat rapidly down the hill in a very disorganised manner.

8.

The fire from our left held up the pursuit but a small party of Germans appeared to be issuing from wood in H. 25.a. and these brought a reverse fire to bear on our position. At the same time our right again began to waver and men began retiring from our position in front of the redoubt. I rallied a party of stragglers and put them in a support line running E.N.E. and W.S.W. through G. 36 d.65 (approx) and a further line in a trench ~~covering~~ curving round the houses South of the LOOS-HILL 70 trench. I left this under the command of an officer (E. Yorks or K.O.Y.L.I.) with orders to hold on at all costs .

The retirement(?) on the left continued rapidly so I endeavoured to form a line along the LOOS-HULLUCH road.

The men however were very hard to stop and I only succeed in placing a garrison of one sergt. and 16 men in the houses at G. 30 c. 53, which had been partly prepared for defence. and a short line on either side under a subaltern of the SOMERSETS.

Two enemy machine guns were in action at the time from about N.E. probably edge of wood at G. 30.d.99 Seeing a Brigadier General (name and Brigade unknown) I reported to him and was ordered to get back to German front system and try to rally troops on their reserve line. Near this line I met another Brigadier (Wilkinson I believe, but am not sure, not 44th Brigade) who ordered me to rally some troops who were moving back to the South of us. I attempted this and got a good number into our front line trench. They were difficult to control and afraid of the Gas which was bad at the time both from German shells and probably leaking cyclinders in our trenches.

About 12.15 p.m. I sent a report to 46th Inf. Bde Headquarters and as situation improved and I was feeling the effects of the gas I went there about 12.45 p.m. to report.

NOTE   During the retirement a large number of Gas Shells were in use and I am not quite certain of the sequence of events.

During the afternoon I assisted in rallying the troops who were retiring and in getting them to man the German Reserve and Fire trenches and our Front and Support trenches .

No 4 Section reported to me and also the Section Officer of one of the 74th Field Co.R.E. . I directed both to assist in the conversion of the German trenches.

27.9.15. At Company Headquarters preparing for return of company.

I would like to bring forward the name of Captain Grant , 10th Bn Sco. Rif., for recognition of his services , his courage energy and capability are of a high order. I also consider that Sapper Jones is deserving of a "Mention in despatches " he was of great assistance to me in rallying troops both during the retirement and afterwards in our lines.

I regret that my noted and time diary are not
available nor copies of messages sent or received,
as my A.B. 153 was dropped and lost on Hill 70.

                                            (Sgd) C.E. Sayer,

28.3.15.   Captain R.E.

"A" Form.
MESSAGES AND SIGNALS. No. of Message

Prefix	Code	m.	Words	Charge	This message is on a/c of:	Recd. at	m.
Office of Origin and Service Instructions.			11			Date	**K**
			Sent		Service.	From	
		At	m.			By	
		To					
		By		(Signature of "Franking Officer.")			

TO — The Brigade Major
                       26th J.B.

* Sender's Number	Day of Month	In reply to Number	AAA
C 399	3rd		

I enclose reports as follows.
aaa Work done by 91st
Field Coy during 24th to
27th aaa Work done by
H Coy 9th Gordon Highlanders
during 24th to 27th aaa.
A copy of Capt. Sayers
report referred to in para
9 of my report has
already been sent to you.

                                     Major R.E.

From — O.C. 91st Field Coy R.E.
Place — VAULX COURT
Time — 10.10 am

The above may be forwarded as now corrected. (Z)

Censor. Signature of Addressor or person authorised to telegraph in his name
* This line should be erased if not required.

91st Field Coy R.E.

1.

Report by Major H. Pollard Lowsley C.I.E. R.E. OC 91st Field Coy. R.E. on the operation of the 24th to 27th Sept 1915.

Reference 10,000 French Map. 36C. NW sheet 39 part of 1.

1. Distribution of Company. In accordance with 46th I.B. order No. 11 dated 15.9.15 the 91st Field Coy R.E. and H Coy of the 9th Gordon Highlanders (Pioneers) were distributed as follows:—

   No. 1 Section 91st Coy (LIEUT. DAVENPORT R.E.) with No. 16 Platoon IX Gordons (2nd LT. MacGREGOR) reserve to No. 3 Column.

   No. 2 Section 91st Coy (LIEUT. McCOURT R.E.) with No. 14 Platoon IX Gordons (2nd LT. BISSET) reserve to No. 4 Column.

   No. 3 Section 91st Coy (LIEUT. MacNAUGHT R.E.) with No. 13 Platoon IX Gordons (2 LT MURRAY) with No. 3 Column.

   No. 4 Section 91st Coy (LIEUT. PARKER. R.E.) with No. 15 Platoon IX Gordons (2LT PITCAIRN) with No. 4 Column.

Capt A.P. SAYER. R.E. (91st Field Coy R.E.) & Capt MacWHIRTER O.C. H Coy 9th Gordons were posted with Nos 1 & 2 sections & their attached Platoons with the Reserve. Major Pollard Lowsley C.I.E. R.E. was, under the orders of B.J. MATHESON, (G.O.C. 46th I.B.) attached to the Brigade H.Q.

The H.Q of the Company with all Wagons ready loaded were located at LE SAULCHOY FARM in MAZINGARBE under C.S.M. NOLAN.
All horses were left in charge of Sergt Linde. at NŒUX LES MINES.

2. <u>Movements</u>. Under the original orders of the G.O.C. 46th I.B. Nos 1 & 2 Sections with their attached platoon of 9th Gordons were due to enter NORTHERN U.P. trench at MAZINGARBE at 7.30 p.m. on the 24th Sept and Nos. 3 & 4 sections & their Platoons at 9.15 p.m. At 6. P.M. on the 24th orders were received to stand fast. At 8.30 pm orders were recd to carry on & times of starting were fixed. Nos 1 & 2 sections 91st Field Coy RE & Nos 14 & 16 Platoons of the 9th Gordons left MAZINGARBE at 9.30 pm with Capt MACWHIRTER & under the command of Capt A.E. Doyer RE. They marched overland to PHILOSOPHE when they entered NORTHERN. U.P. and proceeded to their allotted position in C.T No 16. Nos 3 & 4 sections of the 91st Field Coy RE. with Nos 13 and 15 Platoons 9th Gordons followed at 10.45 pm & took up their position in CTs 15 and 16 respectively

3. At 4.5 am on the 25th Sept the O.C 91st Field Coy RE received information from the 46th I.B. that the gas discharge would commence at 5.50 am

3.

and that the assault would take place at 6.30.
"a.m". These orders were communicated to all Section
Officers who informed Platoon Officers 9th Gordons
Consequent on the change in the time for the
assault it became necessary to alter starting times
for Sections & Platoons. Times were altered to the
following & communicated to Capt SAYER for Nos 1
& 2 Sections & their attached Platoons and to the
Section Officers of Nos 3 & 4 Sections direct

   Nº 3 Section 5.47 a.m.
    — 4 —   5.53 a.m.
    — 1 & 2 — 6.45 a.m.

Times of starting of 8th KOSBs (cols 3 & 4) were also
communicated to Section Officers of Nos 1 & 2 Sections
and these Officers were instructed to arrange their
movements to conform

4. All Sections moved off at the times fixed and all
took up the positions allotted to them in their
Columns. Two parties each consisting of 2 sappers
& 6 Pioneers from Sections 1 & 2 of 9th Coy & Platoons
16 & 14 of the 9th Gordons proceeded to the Russian
Saps in Fire Bays 24 & 131 near Cts. 92 and 9 and
started work with the 2 leading platoons of the
8th KOSBs in each Column, opening up the saps
& continuing them as communication trenches to the
German Front Line trenches. At about 9 a.m.
work on the communication trenches was
inspected by Capt A.R.SAYER.RE who found

4.

an insufficient number of men employed on them. He collected more men, obtained tools for them from near the R.E. trench store No 2 & put them on the work. The work continued & was completed during the day. Work on both trenches was for some time interfered with by snipers & later by shrapnel fire.

5. No 3 Section reached our front parapet at about 7 a.m. & went out with the H.L.I. who were immediately behind them. They came at once under a very heavy fire & lost their Section Officer (LIEUT MAC NAUGHT) badly wounded twice, and all N.C.Os except Lee Cpl. MELVIN R.E. This N.C.O. took forward the remaining men of his section up to the German support trench where he found some Infantry. He set his men to assist the infantry on turning the trenches using such tools as he was able to collect locally. At 10.15 AM. LCE CPL MELVIN reported with the 4 remaining men of his section to Capt SAYER who put SERJT HAY in charge & reported to me that he had done so. The section was then taken by Capt SAYER up towards Hill 70. Acting under Capt SAYER's instructions Serjt Hay reconnoitred a wood running NE from G 30 d.99 7 then commenced to place in a state of defence a barn at G 36 c 89. Tools had to be obtained from H.Q. but by 6 p.m. the barn had been placed in a fair state of defence. About this time an Officer of the A & S Highlanders ordered Serjt Hay

5.

to hand over his tools to his men (A+S H) who
required them to dig themselves in. Serjt HAY
then reported to CAPT SAYER at advanced Brigade
H.Q. for instructions & was instructed to take up
sandbags to the 10th Sco Rifles who were on Hill
70. It was then dark & on his way back to the
R.E Trench store, Serjt Hay lost his party. He reported
this to me at LOOS KEEP about 10 p.m. & I succeeded
in getting into telephonic communication with
some of his men. I sent him up again to find
his men & take up sandbags as he had been
ordered. Serjt Hay failed to find his men that
night but collected five of them early on the
morning of the 26th. As they were all then
exhausted I ordered them to join Section No. 4
in Res Trench 21 & await orders. After that
they ~~formed~~ part of Section 4.

6. No 4 Section (LIEUT. J.A. PARKER) This section reached
C.T. 22 at 6.25 am. on the 25th. Mr Parker then
sent forward two orderlies to the O.C. Col 4 reporting
his position and asking for orders. He received
orders to advance at 6.45 am. The section
proceeded to the firing line via C.T. 22, Support
line 26 & Boyan 9.B. Mr Parker got his men
out at once, extended them along the parapet and
advanced by short rushes towards the German
line. Unfortunately he took a wrong direction,

6.

crossed the Loos Road and entered the zone of N. 5 Column. Two casualties occurred almost immidiately after leaving our trenches. Two more men were hit very soon afterwards, one of them has since died & the other has his leg badly shattered. Eventually by about 7 am the section had reached a point about 50 yds from the German trenches at about G.22 d.42. There they were subjected to an extremely heavy fire & were unable to advance. They endeavoured to advance but eight or nine of the remaining men were hit at once & a few only got as near as within 12-15 yards off the German wire. Mr Parker sent back a message to me informing me of the position and asking for instructions. I received this message from Spr Harlen at about 10 am. I immediately instructed Mr Parker to withdraw his men & proceed to Hill 70, or to join Capt Sayer who was on his right if he could not proceed. Meantime Mr Parker had been busily engaged under very heavy fire in applying first aid dressings to all his wounded men. He did this entirely unaided and continually exposed himself in doing it. The slightest movement on the part of his men was followed by fire from the enemy but Mr Parker was not hit. On receipt of my orders Mr Parker withdrew his section

& brought in the remaining wounded to the LOOS ROAD where they were in comparative safety. In order to bring in Cpl Parrish it was neccessary for N² Parker to crawl 10 yards & fetch a Mambré line. This he fastened round Cpl Parrish and round himself & in this manner dragged Cpl Parrish to a safe position. After getting in his section N² Parker returned & helped in a man of the H.L.I or K.O.S.B.o who had been badly wounded. N² Parker has I consider shown the greatest bravery in rescuing the wounded. He kept his section thoroughly in hand under most trying conditions & the discipline was excellent throughout. Having extricated his section and recovered his wounded N² Parker then proceeded with what remained of the section — about 12 men — towards Hill 70. He left his men under Serjt Oates near the LOOS BENIFONTAINE road and went forward to reconnoitre He found LIEUT DAVENPORT with Section 1. near PUITS 14 digging a trench — then and returned to fetch his men. He then found that his men had no tools & decided to take them back to obtain some. N² Parker reported to me at LOOS KEEP about 7.30 p.m. having left his men in Reserve trench 21. In view of the fact that he had so few men left & that these men were thoroughly exhausted he asked permission to leave them

8.

there for the night and this permission I gave. LIEUT PARKER himself though completely worn out went out later at about 10.30 pm to satisfy himself that all his wounded had been brought in.

On the 26th Sept before leaving H.Q. I instructed LIEUT PARKER to keep his men in Res Trench 21 awaiting orders. I did this as I knew that the 21st and 24th Divisions were to advance & did not consider that the section would be able to do any useful work. During the morning the section joined the men of the 98th Field Coy R.E. and were extended with them in our old front line trench. During the afternoon Mr Parker reported to Genl Matheson that he had about 35 men of the 91st Field Coy and acting under his instruction he withdrew his men. I then saw LIEUT PARKER at about 3.30 pm and seeing that he and his men were absolutely exhausted and unlikely to be of any use without rest Instructed them to return to Mazingarbe for rest & food. Thinking that they might be useful as guides I told Lieut Parker to report to the C.R.E. XV Div, who sent him with his men out to collect stragglers. During the night he collected some 200 to 300 stragglers in Quality Street.

7. No 1 Section (LIEUT A.H. DAVENPORT) This section went over the front parapet near C.T. 9 at

about 9.45.am. They appear to have got out of position and were in front of the 8th KOSBs who had taken a wrong turn in the Trenches. The section with No 16. Platoon 1st Gordons advanced fairly quickly to H31. A27 which was reached at about 9.40 am. Here Capt MacWhirter (O.C. H Coy 1st Gordons) joined LIEUT DAVENPORT and ordered an advance. At the same time the Col. of the 8th K.O.S.Bs ordered Capt MacWhirter to place in a state of defence a house at H25. A95 - near the chalkpit. LIEUT DAVENPORT took his section to carry out this work though it was entirely out of this area. The section stopped at this house for some time (three or four hours) and carried out the following work:-

(1). Demolished a timber outhouse
(2). Constructed 3. M.G. positions to fire from the house facing N. S. and E
(3). Loopholed a wall to fire to the East
(4). Blocked up two windows
(5). Shored up floor over one M.G. emplacement.

At about 1 pm having completed the above work the section with 2 sections of 8th KOSBs dug in on the West side of the LENS Benifontaine road south of the house above refered to. During the afternoon whilst digging was in progress the 6th Cameron Highlanders came up and lined the north side of the wood immediately East of POSTS 14 & 15 (from H 25 d 08 to H 25 d 09 about). They were shelled out of this &

10.

about 4 pm when they lined the West side of the Lens-Hulluch road, partly in trenches above referred to & partly in shallow trenches dug by themselves.

At about 3 pm a few sappers of the section made 2 M.G. emplacements to fire through a wall of the yard of a house on the road immediately NE of Point No 14 B15. This house was heavily shelled but the section suffered no casualties,— though they had to leave the house for a time. Between 5 pm & 6 pm the 2nd Brigade (Loyal N Lancs) arrived & took over the trenches between Points 14 B15 and the Chalkpit.

At 6.30 PM. Lieut Davenport received orders from Capt MacWhirter to fill the gap between H25 d13 and the house @ H31 b29 immediately North of the Lens-Hulluch Road — No 1 Section & No 16 Platoon 1/6 Gordons both dug in there having connection with the 6th Camerons on the right & a miscellaneous force — mostly Camerons, on the left.

At 9 pm. Col Douglas Hamilton gave Capt MacWhirter orders to advance across the Lens-Hulluch road & dig in on the other side. There was not room for both the Pioneers & the Sappers in the new line so the Pioneers dug on the new line & the Sappers dug in about 20 yds in rear of them. They finished digging in @ about midnight. They then rested till 3.30 am on the

11.

26th when Capt MacWhirter gave the order to stand by. At about 5 am on the 26th some of the shell from our heavy guns appeared to fall short at about H31 d28 and Lieut Davenport reports that our Infantry about this point showed signs of wavering. The left stood firm & shouted to them not to give way & no retreat took place. After this nothing of importance happened actually on the line occupied by No 1 Sec & No 16 Platoon until 11. am. When a rapid retirement took place on our left front from the direction of BoisHugo. Lieut Davenport could not see any reason for this retirement but all the same the word to RETIRE was passed down from the left of the line. No 1 Sec & No 16 Platoon did not retire until all the troops had moved. They then retired to the Loos Benifontaine road & lined the East edge of this road which is in cutting. Lieut Davenport did his best to stop retiring troops @ this road but with but little success. After a short pause & seeing that it was useless to stop any longer on this road Lieut Davenport who still had most of his section & a few Pioneers with him retired to the old German Trenches along the Grenay-Benifontaine Road which he reached @ about 11.45 A.M. Here he met the Colonel of the Durham Light Infantry who told him that this road must be held at all

12.

Cost Lieut Davenport assisted him to collect about 200 men in the German trench along the Grenay Benifontaine road. This trench was held under considerable shell fire, but was never attacked by Infantry. When the retreating Infantry of the 21st & 24th Divisions had been collected & brought up in line to Hill 70 - Lieut Davenport who had then lost all his section with the exception of one N.C.O. & two sappers advanced to the Loos Benifontaine Road to see if he could find any of his section - Failing to do so he reported to the O.C. 91st Field Coy at 4.30 pm. I then put Lieut Davenport & Serjt Robinson on to turn back men to our front line trenches, where they did excellent work up to about midnight. The section was eventually collected on the 27th morning at Mazingarbe.

8. No 2 Section Lieut McCourt. This section advanced over the front parapet with No 14 Platoon of the IX Gordons about 8.15 a.m. on the 25th inst. They left the front line between CT 12 & Boyau g3 & followed the Russian Sap from Bay 24 to the German Front line Trenches. Here Lieut McCourt called a halt & waited for No 14 Platoon which arrived soon afterwards with Capt MacWhirter & Lieut Bissett

13

Capt Mac Whirter gave the order to advance as far as possible. They advanced along a line G.28 b.03. G.30 a.00. G.30 d.06. G.30 d.80 H.31 A.30 to H.31 C.61. This advance was made under rifle fire & some shrapnel fire. The point H.31 C.61 near the crest of Hill 70 was reached at about 9 a.m. Here Lieut McCourt ordered his men to lie down in order to investigate what there might be beyond the crest of the hill. No 14 Platoon also lay down Lieut McCourt sent one man forward to reconoitre and before he returned Lieut Bissett who was somewhat anxious to get on, moved his platoon over the crest. Immidiately Lieut Bissett got over the crest he was subjected to heavy fire & Lieut McCourt has seen nothing of him or his platoon since then Lieut McCourt's man returned with a report to the effect that he could not see the 8th K.O.S.B.s over the ridge & that the enemy was firing heavily on the other side Lieut McCourt advanced his section slightly over the ridge but found the position untenable ~~unsuitable~~ and retired to his former position about 100 yards behind the crest of the hill. Almost immediately after this (about 9.30 am) the Infantry who had proceeded beyond the crest of Hill 70. retired in disorder

14.

They quickly rallied about 50 to 100 yards behind Lieut McCourt's position & he then fell back to their line. Seeing Col Sellar 8th KOSBs in rear of the line Lieut McCourt asked him what he should do with the few men of his section then left with him. Col Sellar instructed him to place his men on his firing line on the left, which he did. During the day the enemy made a few weak attacks which were repulsed without difficulty. Towards the evening - about 4 pm - ammunition began to run short but this was quickly made good. During the afternoon Lieut McCourt's men were employed filling sandbags which they carried with them to improve cover. Soon after dusk reinforcements having arrived Lieut McCourt decided to withdraw his men & arranged with an infantry Officer to have them replaced in the firing line. He then proceeded to the house in Loos G.36 b60 & reported to me but before receiving my reply instructing him to stay where he was, & be prepared to assist with the consolidation of the position on Hill 70, Lieut McCourt had withdrawn to Quality Street, where he arrived at about 5 am on the 26th & reported to the O.C. 74th Field Coy R.E. who phoned to the C.R.E. XX Div for instructions. At 9.30 am on the

15.

26th Lieut McCourt received orders to rejoin his Company with such men as he could collect. He was unable to find the Company & on the advice of Capt Graeme (71st Field Coy RE) he attached his men to that company. I met Lieut McCourt in Quality Street at about 2.15 pm &, seeing that he was pretty well played out, I ordered him to join Lieut Parker & proceed to Mazingarbe & report to the CRE XI Division where I expected he & his men would be of assistance in sending out troops in relief. At about 5 pm Lieut McCourt with Lt Parker commenced collecting stragglers on the Lens road & between them they collected about 500 men up to about 8.30 pm. This section returned to Mazingarbe on the morning of the 27th inst.

9. Capt. Sayer RE.

As stated in para 1 of this report Capt Sayer with Capt MacWhirter (9th Gordons) on the night of the 24th inst were with the reserve. I attach a report by Capt Sayer of the work he did during the attack. It will be seen from this report that Capt Sayer's services were utilised in many & various directions. He, throughout the operations, showed coolness & excellent judgment & was of very material assistance in a number of

16.

difficult situations. This was particularly so on the morning of the 26th inst when Capt Sayer's action was largely instrumental in saving Hill 70 from recapture. Subsequent to this Capt Sayer did excellent work on rallying men on our front line & the old German lines.

10. O.C. 91st Field Coy. As stated in para 1 of this report Major Pollard Lowsley was under the orders of the G.O.C. 46th I.B., attached to the Brigade H.Q. During the 25th inst he was occupied chiefly in dealing with Staff work at Brigade H.Q. Chiefly at the advanced H.Q. at the junction of C.T. 22 & Support trench 26. On the morning of the 26 inst he proceeded with the G.O.C. & Staff to the advanced H.Q. @ G 29. b35. At about 11 A.M. when the retirement was in progress he was ordered back by the G.O.C. to the advanced H.Q. at the Junction of C.T. 22 & support trench 26. On the way he went round to collect stragglers & place them in our firing line & supports line & succeeded in collecting about 40 to 50. He then proceeded with Genl. Matheson to Mazingarbe to the Divl. H.Q. & on return continued to assist in collecting troops in the front line. In the evening he proceeded with the G.O.C. to inspect the

German first line trenches & see that they
were properly occupied

11. Recommendation. I wish specially to
mention the following Officers N.C.O.s & men
  Capt A. P. Sayer R.E.
  Lieut A. H. Davenport R.E.
  Lieut J. A. Parker R.E.
 No 44667 Serjt E. A. Robinson
 No 60612 Spr P Harlen
 No 49301 Spr E. A. Abbott
 No 89267 Spr W. Jones

The special actions for which these Officers
N.C.O.s & men are mentioned are detailed
on A.F. W 3121.

12. Work done by the Company. It is clear from
this report that very little sapper work has
been done by the Company in the Operations.
The only section which did any work
worth mentioning was No 1. Sections 3 & 4
were so badly knocked about at the start
that they never had a chance to do anything
The casualties in the two sections numbered
21, and 16 within a few hours of the
commencement of operations & they then
almost ceased to exist as sections. Section
2 became so disorganised after the retreat
of the Infantry on the morning of the 25th

18.

inst from beyond Hill 70 that it was practically impossible for them to do much on the night of the 25th/26th inst when, had they been intact, they might have been of the greatest assistance in organising the defence of Hill 70. The Company displayed a high standard of discipline & no man returned without his arms & equipment, though some slight deficiencies in equipment occurred. The total casualties amount to one Officer & 53 other ranks, out of 6 Officers and 148 other ranks who went into action. The comparatively light casualties I attribute entirely to the excellent Handling of their men by Section Officers, particularly in the case of No. 1. Section, which section was the only one to do any appreciable amount of Sapper work & the casualties in which numbered three only.

Tom Worthington
Major
O.C. 91st Field Coy. R.E.

Haillicourt
29/9/15.
10.30 p.m.

11. 9/GORDON HIGHLANDERS (Pioneers).

9th Gordons

From
    Colonel W. A. Scott, C.B.,
        Commanding 9th Gordon Highlanders, (Pioneers).

To
    Headquarters,
      15th Division.

    I have the honour to report on the part taken by the Battalion under my command in the fighting which took place round LOOS on 25th, 26th and 27th September, 1915.

    It will be necessary for me to divide the account into four parts, as the battalion was split up.-

    1.   The part taken by Headquarters and "E" and "F" Companies.
    2.   "G" Company which was attached to the 44th Brigade.
    3.   "H" Company which was attached to the 46th Brigade.
    4.   The Machine Gun Sections attached to 44th Brigade.

1.   Headquarters and two Companies were ordered to move from NOEUX-LES-MINES to MAZINGARBE on night of 24th September. At 1 p.m. on 25th September I received an order from Headquarters, 15th Division, - "Proceed with your two Companies at once to LOOS and place it in a state of defence." The two Companies under my command moved off at 1.40 p.m., each man carrying a pick or shovel and 6 sandbags.

    As the BETHUNE - LENS road was being shelled I took a road running South of it, leaving QUALITY STREET and FOSSE 7 on my left (AUCHY - LENS Sheet). On reaching the ridge the Battalion came under shell fire. I ordered the Platoons to extend to three paces and follow one another at 200 paces, the centre of each platoon to move along the road and on reaching LOOS to close and take cover. This was done with very few casualties, though the battalion was shelled the whole way. We reached LOOS at 4.15 p.m. It was being shelled.

    Leaving the Companies under cover I went through LOOS to reconnoitre and decided that the East side was the position requiring first attention, as North of it there appeared to be a gap in our line. I could not see where the Right of the next Division was.

    Headquarters was placed in the main street where it bifurcates, the Northern road led to CITE ST. AUGUSTE, the Southern to LENS, (Sheet 36a, Central). "F" Company I settled should place the building round Figure 36 on the left side of the LENS road in defence. "E" Company to make two houses on CITE ST. AUGUSTE road into a keep, and connect with "F" by trenches and prolong the trenches to North of road with the Left flank slightly thrown back. This position supported the Left of the Front Line on/

on HILL 70 and might prevent the left flank from being turned.

On going back to the Companies Captain Robertson reported he examined some houses and had found 20 German soldiers in them. They were sent to PHILOSOPHE under escort.

At 5 p.m. the Companies were ordered to their different positions. Work could not begin till dark on account of the shelling. During the night this work was completed. Continuous shelling went on throughout the night with intermittent bursts of machine gun fire.

Early in the morning I came to the conclusion the situation was critical, the left flank being entirely unguarded; no British Troops could be seen to the North and Germans were firing from PUIT NO. 14 bis and the copse to the North-West (25A). I therefore deemed it advisable not to continue with the defence of LOOS and ordered the two Companies to man their defensive positions. During the morning the shelling of LOOS was very heavy and considerable numbers of wounded were coming back from HILL 70, and more and more fire was coming from the left. At about 1 p.m., I think it was, I noticed German guns shelling the ridges to my left rear where our first line trenches were. I was much relieved shortly afterwards to see two battalions in extended order coming up on our left. They came a certain way and then turned round and retired. I then managed to find out that Brigadier-General Wallenstein, Commanding 45th Brigade, was in LOOS. I went and saw him and explained the dangerous situation on the left and that it appeared to me from the machine gun fire that the Germans were getting more round the left, and that a considerable number of unwounded men were coming back. The bombardment of LOOS had also become very violent. He told me to hang on, as a Battalion was on its way up to support us. They never arrived.

At 3 p.m. I sent the following message to Major MacGregor, - "Hold on all you can; if forced to retire, do so on German first line trenches. I am sending up ammunition. Communicate with Captain Robertson."

I and Headquarters had to retire down the street to a big building which appeared to be a German Store, as the house I had been in was knocked nearly flat. At about 4 p.m. I found I could not get in touch with my two Companies. It appears that some officer in the front line had given the order to "Retire." Afterwards the Officer Commanding "E" Company reported to me that a man dressed as a Sergeant of the A. & S. Highlanders had come to him and given him verbal orders to retire from the Brigade. He said another man had been sent to the first line and asked how he could get there in case the first man failed. Just after he said this there was a backward movement from HILL 70 and this man then said "That is all right, he has got there and they are retiring." The

Companies/

3.

Companies then retired. At this time LOOS was a perfect hell of shell and machine gun fire, all the streets from the North were being enfiladed. I could not find the Brigadier, and as I could do nothing more I, with Headquarters, retired. I ordered the men to follow me in single file at 3 paces, and by hugging the lee side of the street we managed to get to the trenches with the loss of 1 man killed and 3 wounded.

Major MacGregor, after the two Companies got to the trenches, thought that the order to retire was wrong, and as the fire had considerably modified he ordered the two Companies to advance and re-occupy the trenches. This was successfully performed and the firing almost ceased.

At 8 p.m. they were reinforced by a dismounted regiment of Cavalry, of the 3rd Cavalry Division. They remained with the Cavalry all night and were withdrawn from action on Monday morning.

2. REPORT BY OFFICER COMMANDING "G" COMPANY, ATTACHED TO 44TH BRIGADE.

To- Colonel Scott, C.B.,
    Commanding 9th Gordon Highlanders.

Sir,

I have the honour to report the following facts concerning the work done by the Company under my command during the operations September 25th - 27th.

1. In accordance with orders received two Platoons, Nos. 11 and 12, under command of 2nd Lieut. K. B. Kershaw and 2nd Lieut. J. Usher, proceeded on the night of September 24/25th to trenches in the front line, with instructions to follow the rear Companies of the 9th Black Watch and 8th Seaforth Highlanders respectively, as part of the assaulting column.

The other two platoons were ordered to follow in rear of the last Battalion of the 44th Brigade.

Company Headquarters with Brigade Headquarters.

2. No. 11 Platoon followed the 6th or 7th line of the Black Watch. Seeing that the left flank of the Black Watch was exposed, Lieut. KERSHAW led his platoon half left and took some German trenches immediately on the left of the Black Watch. At this time the Black Watch had not yet reached the German first line trenches and were under a hot fire from Machine Guns, Rifles and Bombs.

The second line was captured without opposition and an advance made on LOOS.

Within/

Within 300 yards of LOOS where a road crosses the front a hot fire was encountered from Machine Guns. Lieut. KERSHAW was killed at this point, after having been previously wounded in the arm. All accounts agree that this Officer performed most gallantly in leading that part of the line to the assault on LOOS.

Sergeant FINDLAY then led the platoon into LOOS, where, with the aid of a very gallant Cameron Highlander who threw bombs, a house was captured from which machine gun fire was coming, and 40 or 50 Germans forced to surrender.

The platoon then advanced on to HILL 70 which they helped to consolidate.

3. No. 12 Platoon followed behind the Seaforth Highlanders till within 200 yards of LOOS. As by this time they had 12 casualties and the front line was held up at the barbed wire, Lieut. USHER joined the firing line. LOOS was stormed. In the town Lieut. USHER found several civilians and at once sent them back under escort to QUALITY STREET. LOOS being taken an advance was made on HILL 70. HILL 70 was passed and the line advanced some 500 yards beyond the redoubt almost to CITE ST. AUGUSTE. Lieut. USHER did very good work here showing a fine example of fearlessness under a hot enfilade fire.

Eventually the line there was forced to retire as the right had been driven back. During this retirement while fighting a rear-guard action the platoon lost heavily, Lieut. USHER being killed. On HILL 70 he was as cool as if he was on parade, cheering up the men in every way. He stopped one retirement, and had supports arrived in time HILL 70 would have been saved. Sergeant McKIMMIE took over command and retired with the few men left through the redoubt. He then did some excellent work bringing up tools and wire from a German store in LOOS to the firing line and issueing them to troops passing through. He then dug a line between the two roads going over HILL 70 with the aid of some leaderless men, which line eventually became part of the line held that night.

4. Nos. 9 and 10 Platoons under Lieut. ROBERTSON-DURHAM and Lieut. STEEDMAN, after the assaulting column had gone on, started to open up the new saps from the front line to the enemy's line, under a heavy shell fire. Both platoons lost heavily during this, losing 20% of their men.

They were ordered then to follow behind the 10th Gordon Highlanders and eventually reached HILL 70. Both the platoons passed the redoubt and when the first line retired Lieut. STEEDMAN held on to the redoubt with a mixed lot of men for some considerable time.

Lieut./

Lieut. ROBERTSON-DURHAM did good work consolidating and strengthening the reverse slope of the hill after the redoubt was lost, and when found on the extreme left had his men dug in and sentries posted. He crossed over from the right to the left on their retirement from the top of HILL 70, considering rightly that that was the exposed and therefore dangerous flank.

The Company was ordered by the General Officer Commanding, 44th Brigade, to be withdrawn at 5 p.m., and this was accomplished by the Officer Commanding Company after the line had been re-organized under cover of darkness. The Company passed through LOOS about 10 p.m. and, Brigade Headquarters having been withdrawn to QUALITY STREET, was taken back to that point, some 60 strong, where it went into Brigade Reserve.

Next day at 3 p.m. orders were received to hold the original support line trenches, and next day, September 27th, the company was withdrawn with the rest of the battalion and the 44th Infantry Brigade to MAZINGARBE.

The Company went into action some 203 strong and its casualties were :-

    Killed   - 8 Other Ranks and 2 Officers.
    Wounded - 73 Other Ranks.
    Wounded and
    Missing - 7 Other Ranks.
    Missing - 25 Other Ranks. *

    TOTAL   - 113 Other Ranks and 2 Officers. @

* Mostly hit beyond HILL 70.

@ 2nd Lieut. KERSHAW and 2nd Lieut. ROBERTSON-DURHAM.

3.   "H" Company lost all its Officers and senior Sergeants; only 2 Sergeants came out of action unwounded. The senior Sergeant, Sergeant Merry, compiled these notes. :-

"H" Company, 9th Gordon Highlanders, (Pioneers).

Report by Sergeant MERRY.

On the morning of the 25th the Company was divided as follows-

No. 13 Platoon, under 2nd Lieut. Murray, was attached to 10th Scottish Rifles.

No. 14 Platoon, under 2nd Lieut. Bisset, was ordered to support/

support No. 13 Platoon.

No. 15 Platoon, under 2nd Lieut. PITCAIRN, was attached to 7th King's Own Scottish Borderers.

No. 16 Platoon, under 2nd Lieut. MACGREGOR, was ordered to support No. 15 Platoon.

Each Platoon was ordered to proceed to the Fire Trench by a different route, but on arrival there, owing to some slight confusion, each platoon at once became a fighting unit and attached itself to the nearest line and advanced with them to German first line of trenches. 2nd Lieut. PITCAIRN was wounded just before reaching the German trench, and his Platoon, No. 15, suffered very severely about the same time. The remainder of the Company continued the advance with the nearest unit in the direction of HILL 70.

About this point Captain MACWHIRTER, finding the line again getting into confusion, re-organized the remainder of 15 and 16 Platoons and men of other Corps in his immediate vicinity, and named them 9th Gordons and took command of same.

At the same time 2nd Lieut. MURRAY performed a similar service in his part of the line and placed them in charge of Sergeant MERRY.

2nd Lieut. MURRAY seeing that there were no officers in charge of the line in front of him, went forward and took charge and advanced with them to reinforce the firing line.

Captain MACWHIRTER's command continued the advance until it reached the LA BASSEE - LENS road, where they were ordered to dig themselves in. This happened at about 4 p.m., but at 8 p.m. they were ordered to advance North along the road for about 500 yards and again dig in and to hold that position. This was held till about 11 a.m. on the 26th.

About this time Captain MACWHIRTER, seeing the troops on his right and also some of the 15th Division on his left were retiring, rallied his men and encouraged them to hold on and try to cover the retirement. The enemy then concentrated their machine gun and rifle fire on this party and forced them to retire. This was carried out at a steady pace under orders of Captain MACWHIRTER, during which Captain MACWHIRTER was wounded in the hand. 2nd Lieut. MACGREGOR was killed and Sergeant BLACK and Sergeant MITCHELL were wounded.

The line again became confused owing to the enemy's heavy fire, but as soon as cover was reached Corporal MCCULLY gathered as many men of the 9th Gordons as he could find and was then ordered by General WILKINSON to report to Captain TAYLOR at Headquarters in QUALITY STREET.

The/

7.

The men under command of 2nd Lieut. MURRAY, supported by Sergeant MERRY's command, continued to advance over HILL 70, but were forced to retire to a bank about 250 yards in rear, where they remained until reinforced. During this retirement there was again much confusion, but Captain LONGMAN of the 10th Gordons, assisted by Lieuts. STEEDMAN and ROBERTSON-DURHAM, Company Sergt-Major ERRIDGE and Sergt. ROBSON, checked the retirement and re-organized the line.

Shortly afterwards 2nd Lieut. MURRAY rejoined the line and again retold off in sections and commenced to dig in. During this time 2nd Lieut. MURRAY was wounded across the back by a machine gun bullet, but he remained with his command until he saw that every man was safely dug in, when he handed over to Sergeant MERRY, he then retiring to the Dressing Station.

This party then remained in this position until about 10 p.m. when they were ordered to retire and report to Captain TAYLOR, this being carried out without further loss. The total strength of this company then gathered together by Sergeant MERRY numbered 30 N.C.O's and men.

4. MACHINE GUN SECTIONS.

It is extremely difficult to find out exactly the part taken by the Machine Guns of the Battalion as Lieut. ALLAN, the Machine Gun Officer, was killed on the East side of HILL 70 and all the N.C.O's were killed or wounded.

At first they were ordered to occupy SAP 18 and bring fire on the LENS road redoubt, after the capture of which they were to move forward and act as circumstances occurred. After leaving SAP 18 they went forward through LOOS and came into action on HILL 70 on the crest of the hill, having the German Redoubt on their left. They then advanced again and came into action at close range of CITE ST. AUGUSTE, this was about 9.30 a.m. About 1.30 p.m. the line was forced to retire. It is believed that Lieut. ALLAN was killed here, as he could not be found, and Sergeant WATSON gave the order to retire. They were nearly the last to go. The men crawled back extended, with the guns dismantled. They appear to have made another stand on the East side of HILL 70. Sergeant MACDOWALL, who appears to have been with the reserve section went forward to see the situation. He never returned and the Machine Guns and their gunners were never seen on the West side of the hill. It is believed that the guns were destroyed and the gunners with them killed or wounded in retiring over the crest. Corporal MACKAY, though severely wounded, continued to take up ammunition to the guns. He was last seen lying by the road on West side of HILL 70. After the guns were lost the remainder of the section and reserve section were employed as riflemen.

It/

8.

It has been brought to my notice by several officers that the Machine Gun Section, under Lieut. ALLAN and Sergeant WATSON, fought and behaved in a most exemplary manner; they fought their guns until both guns and gunners were wiped out.

...........................Colonel,
Commanding 9th Gordon Highlanders,
(Pioneers).

1st October, 1915.

www.ingramcontent.com/pod-product-compliance
Lightning Source LLC
Chambersburg PA
CBHW081401160426
43193CB00013B/2085